A Second Supplementary Catalog of Early Wind Band and Wind Ensemble Repertoire

Books by David Whitwell

Philosophic Foundations of Education
Foundations of Music Education
Music Education of the Future
The Sousa Oral History Project
The Art of Musical Conducting
The Longy Club: 1900–1917
A Concise History of the Wind Band
Wagner on Bands
Berlioz on Bands
Chopin: A Self-Portrait
Schumann: A Self-Portrait in His Own Words
Mendelssohn: A Self-Portrait in His Own Words
La Téléphonie and the Universal Musical Language
Extraordinary Women
Aesthetics of Music in Ancient Civilizations
Aesthetics of Music in the Middle Ages
Aesthetics of Music in the Early Renaissance

The History and Literature of the Wind Band and Wind Ensemble Series

Volume 1 The Wind Band and Wind Ensemble Before 1500
Volume 2 The Renaissance Wind Band and Wind Ensemble
Volume 3 The Baroque Wind Band and Wind Ensemble
Volume 4 The Wind Band and Wind Ensemble of the Classical Period (1750–1800)
Volume 5 The Nineteenth-Century Wind Band and Wind Ensemble
Volume 6 A Catalog of Multi-Part Repertoire for Wind Instruments or for Undesignated Instrumentation before 1600
Volume 7 Baroque Wind Band and Wind Ensemble Repertoire
Volume 8 Classical Period Wind Band and Wind Ensemble Repertoire
Volume 9 Nineteenth-Century Wind Band and Wind Ensemble Repertoire
Volume 10 A Supplementary Catalog of Wind Band and Wind Ensemble Repertoire
Volume 11 A Catalog of Wind Repertoire before the Twentieth Century for One to Five Players
Volume 12 A Second Supplementary Catalog of Early Wind Band and Wind Ensemble Repertoire
Volume 13 Name Index, Volumes 1–12, The History and Literature of the Wind Band and Wind Ensemble

www.whitwellbooks.com

David Whitwell

A Second Supplementary Catalog of Early Wind Band and Wind Ensemble Repertoire

THE HISTORY AND LITERATURE OF THE WIND
BAND AND WIND ENSEMBLE, VOLUME 12

EDITED BY CRAIG DABELSTEIN

WHITWELL PUBLISHING · AUSTIN, TEXAS, USA

Whitwell Publishing, Austin 78701
www.whitwellbooks.com

Printed in the United States of America

PAPERBACK
ISBN-13: 978-1-936512-54-6
ISBN-10: 1936512548

Composed in Bembo Book

Contents

Foreword

THIS VOLUME IS THE TWELFTH in the series, *The History and Literature of the Wind Band and Wind Ensemble*, comprised of the following volumes:

The supplementary sources for early band and ensemble repertoire listed here represent my continuing study in European libraries between 1990 and 2000.

The symbols representing specific libraries are those given by R.I.S.M. Their free online catalog, which may be found under 'R.I.S.M. Library Sigla,' will also provide the reader with the location and mailing address for the individual libraries.

The actual shelf-marks given in the present catalog, as well as the spelling of the composer's name and the composition are as they appear in the library catalog where the material is housed.

David Whitwell
Austin, Texas

Instrumentation Code

As an abbreviation for wind instrumentation I use a code of 0000-0000, representing:
flute, oboe, clarinet, bassoon - trumpet, horn, trombone, tuba.

Thus:

3000-	means a work for three flutes
-204	means a work for two trumpets and four trombones
1-1; 2 cornetts	means bassoon, trumpet, and two cornetts.

Text Abbreviations

MS	Manuscript
EP	Early Print
MP	Modern Print (after 1900)
G5	Grove, *Dictionary of Music* (5th edn)
JH	Private research by Janet Heukeshoven, Winona, MN
MGG	*Die Musik in Geschichte und Gegenwart*, Blume, ed. (Kassel: Bärenreiter, 1949–1968)

Acknowledgments

The reader is indebted for the second edition of this book
to Mr. Craig Dabelstein of Brisbane, Australia. Without his
contribution to design and all things involved as an editor this
book would never again have been available.

David Whitwell
Austin, 2012

Supplementary Hautboisten Repertoire

RENAISSANCE SOURCES

Ouvrard, René

[Two curious Renaissance Treatises]
L'Art et la science des nombres
EP   (Paris: Roulland et Ballard, 1677)
    F:Pn (L.10.088)

Secret pour composer en musique par un art nouveau ... par R. O., Maistre de Musique
EP   (Paris: Alliot et Clement, 1660)
    F:Pn (Res. 891)

BAROQUE SOURCES

Lully, Jean-Baptiste (French composer, 1632–1687)

Les airs de Trompettes, timbales et hautbois faits par M. de Lully par Ordre du Roy pour le Carouzel ... 1686
MS F:Pn (Cons. D. 7227)
    This was music for the king's horse ballet.

Philidor l'ainé André-Danican (French composer, 1726–1795)

Pièces de Trompettes et Timbales à 2, 3 & 4 parts.
MS F:Pn (Res. 920)
    This volume was not included in the Philidor discussion in Vol. 7 of this series.

Partit. Des plus marches
MS F:Pn (Res. F. 671)
    This contains much of the basic march repertoire of Lully.

ADDITIONAL SOURCES FOR HAUTBOISTEN REPERTOIRE

Brawas (Prowo), Pierre (German composer, 1697–1757)

Intrada á 6
202-02
MS   S:L (Engelhart Nr. 420)

Concerto á 6
202-02
MS   S:L (Engelhart Nr. 433) Contains violin parts added later

Concerto, in 3 movements
202-
MS   S:L (Engelhart Nr. 499)

Cheisser (Reinhard Keiser) (German, early eighteenth century, or Rinaldo Casare)

Overture
201-02, taille (English horn)
MS   S:L (Engelhart Nr. 474)

Chelleri, Fortunato (Italian, b. 1668)

Concerto
201-02, 2 violins [probably added later]
MS   S:L (Engelhart Nr. 136)

Sonata
201-
MS   S:L (Engelhart Nr. 125)

Concerto, for 2-2, 2 oboe d'amore
MS   S:L (Engelhart Nr. 486)

Graven (or Grave, or Graun), Karl (German composer, 1703–1759)

Concerto
1-01, oboe d'amore
MS   S:L (Wenster I, Nr. 7)

Concerto
21-I
MS   S:L (Wenster D, Nr. 10)

Heimichen, ?

Sonata
201-
MS S:L (Engelhart Nr. 127)

Hertel, Johann Wilhelm (German, 1727–1789)

Concerto
202-1
MS B:Bc (Wotquenne 7682)

Kegel, A. H.

Overture
2 oboes, taille [English horn], string bass
MS S:L (Wenster L, Nr. 1)

Keller, Gottfried (German composer, d. 1704)

Sainsbury identifies Keller as a celebrated English harpsichordist who published 'five-part sonatas for flutes, hautboys, etc.' at the beginning of the eighteenth century.

Keyser, M. (Baroque composer)

Overture
301-
MS S:L (Wenster L, Nr. 3)

Linike, Johann Georg (German, Baroque composer)

Concerto à 5 in G major
4001-
MS S:L (Kraus Nr. 136)

Mahr, Signr.

Overture à 6
MS S:L (Engelhart Nr. 192) Engelhart has changed 'alto' [taille] to 'viola.'

Marcelo, Alessandro (1684–1750)

MGG attributes to Marcello (12) *Concerti a cinque* (Amsterdam: Roger, 1716) and reproduces a page of the music in Vol. VIII, col. 1616.

Mattheson, Johann (1681–1764)

Overture avec sa Suite, 'pour les hautbois de Mr. le General de Schoulenbourg'
301-02
MS [cited in MGG]

Niedt, Friedrich Erhardt (d. 1717)

Sainsbury identifies Niedt as the composer of *The German Frenchman. Six Suites of Airs*
(Copenhagen, 1708), for 301-, 'composed for the Amusement and Pastime of intelligent
Lovers of the noble Science of Music.'

Rossman, ?

Overture à 5
201-02
MS S:L (Engelhart Nr. 422) 6 movements

Overture
201-02
MS S:L (Engelhart Nr. 473)

Scheer, ?

Concerto
202-
MS S:L (Kraus Nr. 2–4)

Scheidemantel, ?

Sonata in B♭ major
201-
MS S:L (Engelhart Nr. 124)

Schieferdeckern, Johann Christian (German, Baroque composer)

(2) *Concerti* à 4, for
202-
EP (Hamburg: Grefinger, 1713)
S:L (Engelhart 19)
Nr. 11 and 12 contain two pages of interesting introduction … 'for all music lovers.'

Sidow, Samuel (German Baroque composer)

Concerto à 6
302-1, in three movements
MS S:L (Wenster D. Nr. 2)

Simon, Martin

Concerto (1728)
2100-, continuo
MS S:L (Wenster I, Nr. 21)

Taliano (the 'Italiano'?)

Concerto à 6
2101-02
MS S:L (Engelhart Nr. 419)

Telemann, Georg (German, 1681–1767)

Concerto in F major
201-02
MS S:L (Kraus Nr. 142)
  Le Ris
  Les Proles
  Espaniole en Ronddeau
  Fanfare
  The cover reads, 'Overture 100' and the Oboe I part reads 'Overture Nr. 142'

Anonymous

Concerto in F Major, 4 movements
201-02
MS S:L (Engelhart Nr. 519)

Concerto á 6 in B♭ Major, 3 movements
402-
MS S:L (Wenster D, Nr. 25)

Concerto for solo horn
201-
MS S:L (Wenster I, Nr. 4)

Concerto for solo horn, oboe d'amore, bassoon
MS S:L (Wenster I, Nr. 6)

Concerto in D Major (5 movements)
301-1
MS S:L (Engelhart Nr. 383)

Concerto à 6 in F Major
202-02
MS S:L (Engelhart Nr. 415)

Concerto in F Major
201-02, taille [Eng. Hn]
MS S:L (Engelhart Nr. 421)

Concerto à 5 in F Major (6 movements)
201-02
MS S:L (Engelhart Nr. 434)

Concerto à 6 in F Major (6 movements)
202-02
MS S:L (Engelhart Nr. 436)

Intrada in F Major (4 movements)
200-02, taille
MS S:L (Engelhart Nr. 417)

Intrada à 5 in F Major (3 movements)
201-02
MS S:L (Engelhart Nr. 193)

Intrada à 5 in F Major (7 movements)
201-02
MS S:L (Engelhart Nr. 198)

Intrada à 6 in F Major (9 movements)
201-02, taille
MS S:L (Engelhart Nr. 233)

Overture in F Major (5 movements)
202-02
MS S:L (Engelhart Nr. 520)

Overture in F Major (7 movements, including an 'echo' movement)
201-02
MS S:L (Engelhart Nr. 467)

Overture à 5 in F Major (6 movements)
201-02
MS S:L (Engelhart Nr. 418)

Overture
201-
MS   S:L (Engelhart Nr. 389), parts marked 'Violino o Hoboe'

Overture
201-, taille
MS   S:L (Engelhart Nr. 144), contains mss parts arr. for other insts.

Overture à 5 in D Major (8 movements)
201-02
MS   S:L (Engelhart Nr. 250)

Overture de Poste in B♭ Major
201-, post horn
MS   S:L (Engelhart Nr. 372)

Symphonie in D Major (2 movements)
201-2, timpani
MS   S:L (Engelhart Nr. 475) Autograph score with ms violin parts added later

Symphonia in F Major
201-02
MS   S:L (Engelhart Nr. 153)
   Aria
   Allegro
   Larghetto
   Menuet
   Pollonesse
   Pollonesse
   Giga
   Boure
   Menuetto

(12) *Sonaten*
2 oboes, flute douce, continuo
MS   S:L (Engelhart Nr. 692)

[Untitled movement]
201-
MS   S:L (Engelhart Nr. 394)

Concerto in C Major
302-1
MS   D:HRD Fü (3715a)
MP (Hamburg: Sikorski, 1966, as a work by Albinoni, 1671–1751)

Concerto in D Major (5 movements)
302-01
MS D:HRD Fü (3707a)

Concerto in C Major (4 movements)
402-
MS D:HRD Fü (3702a)

Concerto F Major (4 movements)
402-
MS D:HRD Fü (3701a)

Supplementary Harmoniemusik Repertoire

MOST OF THE WORKS LISTED BELOW are from one of the many private aristocratic collections which turn up from time to time, in this case a large group of *Harmoniemusik* works found in the Festetics Palace in Keszthely in Hungary. This collection first came to my attention many years ago when an American bassoonist who had married a Hungarian lady from this town told me of this collection. As he related it, when his young lady brought him to visit her home town he visited the palace, which at that time the Communist had turned into a folk museum. Walking around in a large empty ballroom he noticed a door inconspicuously hidden in the curve of a column and upon opening it found a quantity of original *Harmoniemusik*. He confided this information to me as he had concluded he would never have reason to use this material and knew I was at that time one of very few persons interested in early wind ensemble music. After a few years I knew a friend was going to conduct in that area so I asked him to see if he could find this collection. He did, but lacked the time to write down more than a representative list of compositions. The collection is particularly valuable for the addition of a great number of previously unknown works by Druschetzky and Carlo Kreith.

Finally this collection has been cataloged and much of the collection has been microfilmed by the National Library in Budapest. After the collection had been cataloged a student at the Hochschule für Musik, Graz, as an academic project, compiled a catalog with music incipits which the reader may obtain under the title, Ewald Preinsperger, *Verzeichnis der Noten für Harmonie-Musik and Blasorchester in der Festetics-Sammlung in Keszethely/Ungarn* (Oberschützen: Pannonischen Forschungsstelle, 1993). For the works quoted from this collection the shelfmarks of the original collection in Keszthely follow the letter 'K.' The letter 'H' signifies the shelf-mark of the microfilm copy in the National Library in Budapest.

Anonymous

Grand Partita Turco
2022-12, piccolo, perc.
MS H:K (950/VIII)
    Marsch
    Andante
    Marsch
    Marsch

[5] *Polonessens*
222-02
MS H:K (951/VIII)

Amon, Johann Andreas (German, 1763–1825)

VI Pieces, pour Musique torque [band], Op. 40
202-221, piccolo, 2 E♭ clarinets and percussion
EP   André, Offenbach [Nr. 2233]
   H:K (679/VIII)

Boieldieu, Adrien (French, 1775-1834, 'Maitre de Chapelle de sa Majeste l'Empereur de toutes les Rufsiere et Membre du Conservatoire de Musique de franc')

Six Marches Militaires, 'Dedicated to his Imperial Monseigneur le grand duc Constantin and composed
   for the Musique of his Regiments'
2021-221, Serpent and percussion
EP   Naigueli, Jean George, Zuric
   H:K (2202)

Bonasegla, Carl Philipp (German, b. 1770)

Walzer
2022-12
MS   G:BÜu (13-on-40)

Buhl, Joseph-David (French, 1781–1860, 'Chevalier de la Legion d'honneur, Auteur de l'Ordonnance de Trompette et Ex-Chef de l'Ecole de la Garde Impérale')

Marche du Sacre [changed in a note on the score to '*Fanfare du Sacre*'], 'For the Royal
   Madame la Grande Duchesse Stéphanie de Bade'
E♭ trumpet, saxhorns in E♭, B♭, tenor saxhorn in E♭ and trombone
MS   H:K (2285/X)

Druschetzky, Georg (1745–1819)

Concerto in F
22-02 [first clarinet is called 'Clarinetto Principalo']
MS   H:K (0/147) The folder says 'Nr. 93.'
   H:Bn (FM 4/2029)
   Allegro
   Romance
   Rondo Tempo di Polonese

Concerto in E♭, '*Composée Par Seigneur George Druschezky*'
Solo piano, 22-02
MS H:K (0/139)
    H:Bn (FM 4/2021)
    Allegro
    Andante
    Variazioni & Thema

Concerto in E♭, 'Composée Par Seigneur George Druschezky' [title page] 'Del Sig: Giorgio
    Druschetzky' [on the parts]
MS H:K (0/134) The folder says 'Nr. 12'
    H:Bn (FM 4/2016)
MP Dorottya Somorjay, ed., Budapest, 1985, as Musicalia Danubiana 4
    Allegro
    Romance Andante
    Rondo Nazionale

Divertissement, 32 compositions for 3 bassett horns, 'Composée Par Seigneur
    George Druschezky'
MS H:K (0/120) The folder says 'Nr. 112' and 33 compositions, but Nr. 14 is missing.
    H:BN (FM 4/2002)
MP Bernhard Habla, ed., Kliment Wien
MP Jirí Kratochvil, ed., OTMS Dolní Sytová 1989 [18 of the pieces]

Echo Partie in G, 'Composée Par Seigneur George Druschezky' [title page] 'Del Sig: Gior-
    gio Druschetzky' [on the parts]
22-02
MS H:K (0/137) The folder says 'Nr. 76'
    H:Bn (FM 4/2019)
    Allegro
    Menuetto
    Poco Adagio
    Rondo

Echo Partie in D, 'Composée Par Seigneur George Druschezky' [title page] 'Del Sig: Giorgio Druschetzky' [on the parts]

22-02

MS   H:K (o/143) the folder says 'Nr. 77'
      H:Bn (FM 4/2025)
      Allegro
      Allegro Menuetto
      Andante
      Rondo

Les Danses Paysannes, Pour l'Harmonie, title page says 'Composée Par Seigneur George Druschezky' together with a list of 88 compositions by Druschetzky

22-02 [B♭ alto]

MS   H:K (o/118) Missing the first clarinet part; The folder says 'Nr. 91'
      H:Bn (FM 4/2000)

Partie in A, 'Composée Par Seigneur George Druschezky' [title page] 'Del Sig: Giorgio Druschetzky' [on the parts]

22-02

MS   H:K (o/195) The folder says 'Nr. 26'
      H: Bn (FM 4/2077)
      Allegro
      Menuetto
      Allegretto
      Rondo

Partie in B♭, 'Composée Par Seigneur George Druschezky' [title page] 'Del Sig: Giorgio Druschetzky' [on the parts]

22-02

MS   H:K (o/130) The folder says 'Nr. 8'
      H:Bn (FM 4/2012)

MP   Dorottya Somorjay, ed., Budapest, 1985, as Musicalia Danubiana 4
      Allegro
      Allegretto Menuetto

Andante
Rondo

Partie in B♭, 'Composée Par Seigneur George Druschezky'

22-02

MS   H:K (0/135) The folder says 'Nr. 8'
     H:Bn (FM 4/2017)

MP   Dorottya Somorjay, ed., Budapest, 1985, as Musicalia Danubiana 4

    Allegro assai
    Romance Andante
    Menuetto Allegretto
    Sicilliano Andante
    Menuetto
    Rondo Allegro

Partie in B♭, 'Composée Par Seigneur George Druschezky' [title page] 'Del Sig: Giorgio
   Druschetzky' [on the parts]

22-02

MS   H:K (0/146) The folder says 'Nr. 60'
     H:Bn (FM 4/2028)
    Allegro
    Menuetto
    Andante
    Rondo

Partie in B♭, 'Composée Par Seigneur George Druschezky'

22-02

MS   H:K (0/149) The folder says 'Nr. 12'
    H:Bn (FM 4/2031)
    Allegro Moderato
    Adagio
    Menuetto
    Moderato Rondeau

Partie in B♭, 'Composée Par Seigneur George Druschezky' [title page] 'Del Sig: Giorgio Druschetzky' [on the parts]

22-02

MS   H:K (0/153) The folder says 'Nr. 14'
    H:Bn (FM 4/2035)
    Allegro
    Poco Adagio
    Rondo Andantino

Partie in B♭ 'Composée Par Seigneur George Druschezky' [title page] 'Del Sig: Giorgio Druschetzky' [on the parts]

22-02 [in B♭ alto]

MS   H:K (0/156) The folder says 'Nr. 11'
    H:Bn (FM 4/2038)
    Allegro
    Menuett
    Romance Andante
    Rondo Allegro

Partie in B♭, 'Composée Par Seigneur George Druschezky'[title page] 'Del Sig: Giorgio
     Druschetzky' [on the parts]
22-02 [in B♭ alto]
MS H:K (0/157) The folder says 'Nr. 52'
     H:Bn (FM 4/2039)
     Allegro
     Menuetto
     Adagio
     Rondo

Partie in B♭, 'Composée Par Seigneur George Druschezky' [title page] 'Del Sig: Giorgio
     Druschetzky' [on the parts]
22-02
MS H:K (0/159) The folder says 'Nr. 10'
     H:Bn (FM 4/2041)
     Allegro
     Menuetto
     Andante
     Rondo Allegro

Partie in B♭, 'Composée Par Seigneur George Druschezky' [title page] 'Del Sig. Giorgio
     Druschetzky' [on the parts]
22-02
MS H:K (0/165) The folder says 'Nr. 2'
     H:Bn (FM 4/2047)
     Allegro
     Menuetto poco Allegretto
     Adagio
     Allegro

Partie in B♭, 'Composée Par Seigneur George Druschezky'[title page] 'Del Sig: Giorgio Druschetzky' [on the parts]

22-02 [in B♭ alto]

MS   H:K (0/179) The folder says 'Nr. 38'

H:Bn (FM 4/2061)

Allegro

Menuetto Allegretto

Andante

Allegro

Partie in C, 'Composée Par Seigneur George Druschezky'[title page] 'Del Sig: Giorgio Druschetzky' [on the parts]

22-02 [in B♭ basse & alto]

MS   H:K (0/140) The folder says 'Nr. 80'

H:Bn (FM 4/2022)

Allegro

Romance Moderato

Menuetto Allegretto

Variazioni

Menuetto Fresco

Rondo Allegro

Partie in C, 'Composée Par Seigneur George Druschezky' [title page] 'Del Sig: Giorgio Druschetzky' [on the parts]

20-02 [in B♭ basse & alto]

MS   H:K (0/142) The folder says 'Nr. 71'

H:Bn (FM 4/2024)

Adagio

Andante

Menuetto

Allegro Finale

Partie in C, 'Composée Par Seigneur George Druschezky'
22-02 [in B♭ basse & alto]
MS   H:K (o/145) The folder says 'Nr. 78'
    H:Bn (FM 4/2027)
    Allegro
    Andante
    Menuetto
    Moderato Variazioni
    Allegro rondo

Partie in C, 'Composée Par Seigneur George Druschezky' [title page] 'Del Sig: Giorgio
    Druschetzky' [on the parts]
22-02
MS   H:K (o/154) The folder says 'Nr. 19'
    H:Bn (FM 4/2036)
    Allegro
    Adagio
    Rondo

Partie in C, 'Composée Par Seigneur George Druschezky' [title page] 'Del Sig: Giorgio
    Druschetzky' [on the parts]
22-02 [in B♭ basse & alto]
MS   H:K (o/182) The folder says 'Nr. 30'
    H:Bn (FM 4/2064)
    Allegro
    Menuetto
    Adagio
    Rondo Allegro

Partie in C, 'Composée Par Seigneur George Druschezky' [title page] 'Del Sig: Giorgio
  Druschetzky' [on the parts]
22-02 [in B♭ basse & alto]
MS H:K (0/190) The folder says 'Nr. 81'
  H:Bn (FM 4/2072)
  Allegro
  Menuetto
  Polonese
  Rondo

Partie in D, 'Composée Par Seigneur George Druschezky' [title page] 'Del Sig: Giorgio
  Druschetzky' [on the parts]
22-02 [in B♭ basse & alto]
MS H:K (0/144) The folder says 'Nr. 79'
  H:Bn (FM 4/2026)
  Allegro
  Andante
  Menuetto Allegretto
  Rondo

Partie in D, 'Composée Par Seigneur George Druschezky' [title page] 'Del Sig: Giorgio
  Druschetzky' [on the parts]
22-02 [in B♭ basse & alto]
MS H:K (0/183) The folder says 'Nr. 88'
  H:Bn (FM 4/2065)
  Allegro
  Menuetto Allegro
  Andante poco Adagio
  Rondo

Partie in D, 'Composée Par Seigneur George Druschezky' [title page] 'Del Sig: Giorgio
    Druschetzky' [on the parts]
22-02 [in B♭ basse & alto]
MS H:K (0/192) The folder says 'Nr. 83'
    H:Bn (FM 4/2074)
    Allegro
    Menuetto Allegro
    Romance Andante
    Rondo Presto

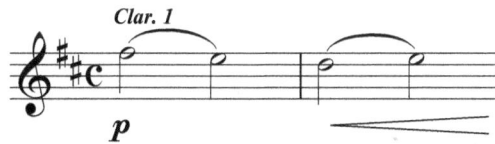

Partie in D, 'Composée Par Seigneur George Druschezky' [title page] 'Del Sig: Giorgio
    Druschetzky' [on the parts]
22-02 [in B♭ basse & alto]
MS H:K (0/193) A note on the part suggests there may have been oboe parts, but there are
    missing here. The folder says 'Nr. 86,' but the parts say 'Nr. 119'
    H:Bn (FM 4/2075)
    Allegro
    Adagio
    Menuetto
    Allegro

Partie in E♭ 'Composée Par Seigneur George Druschezky'
22-02
MS H:K (0/126) The folder says 'Nr. 68'
    H:Bn (FM 4/2008)
MP Dorottya Somorjay, ed., Budapest, 1985, as Musicalia Danubiana 4
    Allegro
    Andante
    Menuetto
    Poco Adagio
    Andante con Variazioni
    Allegretto
    Rondo

Partie in E♭, 'Composée Par Seigneur George Druschezky' [title page] 'Del Sig: Giorgio Druschetzky' [on the parts]

22-02

MS H:K (o/131) The folder says 'Nr. 7'
    H:Bn (FM 4/2013)

MP Dorottya Somorjay, ed., Budapest, 1985, as Musicalia Danubiana 4
    Allegro
    Menuetto
    Adagio
    Rondo

Partie in E♭, 'Composée Par Seigneur George Druschezky' [title page] 'Del Sig: Giorgio Druschetzky' [on the parts]

22-02

MS H:K (o/132) The folder says 'Nr. 4'
    H:Bn (FM 4/2014)

MP Dorottya Somorjay, ed., Budapest, 1985, as Musicalia Danubiana 4
    Allegro
    Menuetto Allegretto
    Andante
    Rondeau Allegro

Partie in E♭, 'Composée Par Seigneur George Druschezky' [title page] 'Del Sig: Giorgio Druschetzky' [on the parts]

22-02

MS H:K (o/136) The folder says 'Nr. 1'
    H:Bn (FM 4/2018)

MP Dorottya Somorjay, ed., Budapest, 1985, as Musicalia Danubiana 4
    Allegro
    Menuetto
    Andante
    Thema con Variazioni

Partie in E♭, 'Composée Par Seigneur George Druschezky' [title page] 'Del Sig: Giorgio Druschetzky' [on the parts]

22-02

MS H:K (0/138) The folder says 'Nr. 16'
>H:Bn (FM 4/2020)
>
>*Allegro*
>
>*Andante Moderato*
>
>*Allegro*
>
>*Menuetto*
>
>*Andante Moderato, Thema mit vier Variationen*

Partie in E♭, 'Composée Par Seigneur George Druschezky' [title page] 'Del Sig: Giorgio Druschetzky' [on the parts]

22-02

MS H:K (0/141) The folder says 'Nr. 69'
>H:Bn (FM 4/2023)
>
>*Allegro*
>
>*Menuetto Allegro*
>
>*Andante*
>
>*Allegro Rondo*

Partie in E♭ 'Composée Par Seigneur George Druschezky' [title page] 'Del Sig: Giorgio Druschetzky' [on the parts]

22-02

MS H:K (0/148) The folder says 'Nr. 24'
>H:Bn (FM 4/2030)
>
>*Allegro*
>
>*Menuetto*
>
>*Andante*
>
>*Allegro*

Partie in E♭, 'Composée Par Seigneur George Druschezky' [title page] 'Del Sig: Giorgio Druschetzky' [on the parts]

22-02

MS   H:K (0/150) The folder says 'Nr. 18' On the back side of these parts is an arrangement by Druschetzky for 22-02 of Mozart's '*Priester Marsch aus der Oper Zauber-Flöte*'

    H:Bn (FM 4/2032)

    Allegro

    Menuetto

    Romance Andante

    Thema Variazioni

Partie in E♭, 'Composée Par Seigneur George Druschezky' [title page] 'Del Sig: Giorgio Druschetzky' [on the parts]

22-02

MS   H:K (0/151) The folder says 'Nr. 44'

    H:Bn (FM 4/2033)

    Allegro

    Menuetto poco Allegretto

    Romance Andante

    Rondo Allegro

Partie in E♭ 'Composée Par Seigneur George Druschezky' [title page] 'Del Sig: Giorgio Druschetzky' [on the parts]

22-02

MS   H:K (0/152) The folder says 'Nr. 17'

    H:Bn (FM 4/2034)

    Allegro

    Menuetto Allegro

    Adagio

    Rondo

Partie in E♭, 'Composée Par Seigneur George Druschezky' [title page] 'Del Sig: Giorgio
  Druschetzky' [on the parts]

22-02

MS   H:K (0/155) The folder says 'Nr. 3'
     H:Bn (FM 4/2037)
     Allegro
     Andante
     Menuetto Allegretto
     Variazioni thema

Partie in E♭, 'Composée Par Seigneur George Druschezky' [title page] 'Del Sig: Giorgio
  Druschetzky' [on the parts]

22-02

MS   H:K (0/158) The folder says 'Nr. 56'
     H:Bn (FM 4/2040)
     Andante moderato
     Menuetto
     Rondo

Partie in E♭, 'Composée Par Seigneur George Druschezky'[title page] 'Del Sig: Giorgio
  Druschetzky' [on the parts]

22-02

MS   H:K (0/160) The folder says 'Nr. 53'
     H:Bn (FM 4/2042)
     Allegro
     Menuetto Allegretto
     Andante
     Rondo

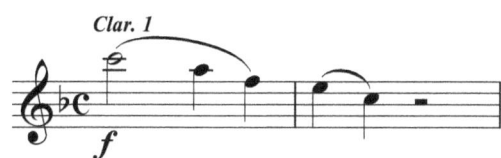

Partie in E♭, 'Composée Par Seigneur George Druschezky' [title page] 'Del Sig: Giorgio Druschetzky' [on the parts]

22-02

MS H:K (0/161) The folder says 'Nr. 59'
    H:Bn (FM 4/2043)
    Adagio
    Menuett
    Romance Andante
    Rondo Allegro

Partie in E♭, 'Composée Par Seigneur George Druschezky' [title page] 'Del Sig: Giorgio Druschetzky' [on the parts]

22-02

MS H:K (0/167) The folder says 'Nr. 54'
    H:Bn (FM 4/2049)
    Allegro
    Menuetto
    Andante
    Rondo

Partie in E♭, 'Composée Par Seigneur George Druschezky' [title page] 'Del Sig: Giorgio Druschetzky' [on the parts]

22-02

MS H:K (0/168) The folder says 'Nr. 20'
    H:Bn (FM 4/2050)
    Allegro
    Menuetto
    Adagio
    Allegro

Partie in E♭ 'Composée Par Seigneur George Druschezky' [title page] 'Del Sig: Giorgio Druschetzky' [on the parts]

22-02

MS H:K (0/170) The folder says 'Nr. 5'
    H:Bn (FM 4/2052)
    Allegro
    Menuetto
    Andante
    Rondo Allegro

Partie in E♭ 'Composée Par Seigneur George Druschezky' [title page] 'Del Sig: Giorgio Druschetzky' [on the parts]

22-02

MS H:K (0/171) The folder says 'Nr. 117'
    H:Bn (FM 4/2053)
    Allegro
    Adagio
    Menuetto Allegretto
    Rondo

Partie in E♭, 'Composée Par Seigneur George Druschezky'[title page] 'Del Sig: Giorgio Druschetzky' [on the parts]

22-02

MS H:K (0/172) The folder says 'Nr. 23'
    H:Bn (FM 4/2054)
    Andante
    Andantino
    Menuetto Allegretto
    Allegro con Variazioni [begins with the 'Jupiter' motiv]

Partie in E♭, 'Composée Par Seigneur George Druschezky' [title page] 'Del Sig: Giorgio
  Druschetzky' [on the parts]

22-02

MS H:K (0/173) The folder says 'Nr. 15'
    H:Bn (FM 4/2055)
    Allegro
    Menuetto
    Andante
    Variazioni

Partie in E♭ 'Composée Par Seigneur George Druschezky' [title page] 'Del Sig: Giorgio
  Druschetzky' [on the parts]

22-02

MS H:K (0/174) The folder says 'Nr. 22'
    H:Bn (FM 4/2056)
    Allegro
    Menuetto Allegro
    Romance Andante
    Rondo con Variazioni

Partie in E♭, 'Composée Par Seigneur George Druschezky'[title page] 'Del Sig: Giorgio
  Druschetzky' [on the parts]

22-02

MS H:K (0/175) The folder says 'Nr. 55'
    H:Bn (FM 4/2057)
    Allegro
    Menuetto
    Andante
    Rondo

Partie in E♭, 'Composée Par Seigneur George Druschezky' [title page] 'Del Sig: Giorgio
    Druschetzky' [on the parts]

22-02

MS H:K (0/176) The folder says 'Nr. 21'
    H:Bn (FM 4/2058)
    Allegro assai
    Adagio cantabile
    Menuetto
    Andante
    Menuetto Allegro
    Allegro Finale

Partie in E♭, 'Composée Par Seigneur George Druschezky' [title page] 'Del Sig: Giorgio
    Druschetzky' [on the parts]

22-02

MS H:K (0/177) The folder says 'Nr. 47'
    H:Bn (FM 4/2059)
    Allegro
    Menuetto Allegretto
    Andante
    Rondo

Partie in E♭, 'Composée Par Seigneur George Druschezky'[title page] 'Del Sig: Giorgio
    Druschetzky' [on the parts]

22-02

MS H:K (0/178) The folder says 'Nr. 90'
    H:Bn (FM 4/2060)
    Allegro
    Menuetto
    Andante
    Rondo Allegro

Partie in E♭, 'Composée Par Seigneur George Druschezky'[title page] 'Del Sig: Giorgio Druschetzky' [on the parts]

22-02

MS   H:K (o/181) The folder says 'Nr. 28'
   H:Bn (FM 4/2063)
   Allegro
   Adagio
   Menuetto Allegretto
   Rondo con Variazioni

Partie in E♭, 'Composée Par Seigneur George Druschezky' [title page] 'Del Sig: Giorgio Druschetzky' [on the parts]

22-02

MS   H:K (o/187) The folder says 'Nr. 50'
   H:Bn (FM 4/2069)
   Allegro
   Menuetto
   Adagio
   Rondo

Partie in E♭, 'Composée Par Seigneur George Druschezky' [title page] 'Del Sig: Giorgio Druschetzky' [on the parts]

22-02

MS   H:K (o/188) The folder says 'Nr. 49'
   H:Bn (FM 4/2070)
   Allegro
   Menuetto
   Andante poco Adagio
   Variazioni Allegro

Partie in E♭, 'Composée Par Seigneur George Druschezky' [title page] 'Del Sig: Giorgio
  Druschetzky' [on the parts]

22–02

MS H:K (0/189) The folder says 'Nr. 48'
  H:Bn (FM 4/2071)
  Allegro
  Menuetto
  Andante
  Rondo

Partie in F, 'Composée Par Seigneur George Druschezky'

22–02

MS H:K (0/127) The folder says 'Nr. 113'
  H:Bn (FM 4/2009)

MP Dorottya Somorjay, ed., Budapest, 1985, as Musicalia Danubiana 4
  Allegro
  Andante poco Adagio
  Menuett Allegretto
  Allegro

Partie in F, 'Composée Par Seigneur George Druschezky' [title page] 'Del Sig: Giorgio
  Druschetzky' [on the parts]

22–02

MS H:K (0/129) The folder says 'Nr. 63'
  H:Bn (FM 4/2011)

MP Dorottya Somorjay, ed., Budapest, 1985, as Musicalia Danubiana 4
  Adagio
  Menuetto
  Rondo Allegro Molto

Partie in F, 'Composée Par Seigneur George Druschezky' [title page] 'Del Sig: Giorgio Druschetzky' [on the parts]

22-02

MS   H:K (0/133) The folder says 'Nr. 9'
      H:Bn (FM 4/2015)

MP   Dorottya Somorjay, ed., Budapest, 1985, as Musicalia Danubiana 4
      Andante Moderato
      Menuetto Allegretto
      Romance Andante
      Rondo Allegro

Partie in F, 'Composée Par Seigneur George Druschezky'

22-02

MS   H:K (0/162) The folder says 'Nr. 58'
      H:Bn (FM 4/2044)
      Allegro
      Menuetto
      Andante
      Rondo

Partie in F, 'Composée Par Seigneur George Druschezky'

22-02

MS   H:K (0/163) The folder says 'Nr. 67'
      H:Bn (FM 4/2045)
      Allegro
      Romana Poco Adagio
      Menuetto
      Variazioni Moderato Thema

Partie in F, 'Composée Par Seigneur George Druschezky'
22-02
MS   H:K (0/164) The folder says 'Nr. 42'
     H:Bn (FM 4/2046)
     Allegro Moderato
     Menuetto Allegretto
     Adagio con Variazioni
     Rondo

Partie in F 'Composée Par Seigneur George Druschezky'
22-02
MS   H:K (0/169) The folder says 'Nr. 6'
     H:Bn (FM 4/2051)
     Allegro
     Romance
     Menuetto allegretto
     Rondo con Thema Variazioni

Partie in F 'Composée Par Seigneur George Druschezky'
22-02
MS   H:K (0/184) The folder says 'Nr. 37'
     H:Bn (FM 4/2066)
     Adagio
     Andante Moderato
     Menuetto Allegretto
     Rondo Allegro

Partie in F, 'Composée Par Seigneur George Druschezky'
22-02
MS H:K (0/185) The folder says 'Nr. 40'
    H:Bn (FM 4/2067)
    Allegro
    Romance Andante
    Menuetto Allegretto
    Rondo

Partie in G, 'Composée Par Seigneur George Druschezky'
22-02
MS H:K (0/180) The folder says 'Nr. 87'
    H:Bn (FM 4/2062)
    Allegro
    Menuetto
    Adagio
    Rondo con Variazioni

Partie in G, 'Composée Par Seigneur George Druschezky'
22-02
MS H:K (0/191) The folder says 'Nr. 82'
    H:Bn (FM 4/2073)
    Allegro
    Menuetto Allegro
    Adagio
    Rondo Presto

Partitta La fantasia, 'Composée Par Seigneur George Druschezky' [title page] 'Del Sig: Giorgio Druschetzky' [on the parts]

22-02

MS   H:K (0/194) The folder says both 'Nr. 25' and '32'

H:Bn (FM 4/2076)

Allegro

Andante – Allegro assai

Menuetto

Adagio

Andante bzw. Allegro

Allegro

Serenade in E♭ 'Composée Par Seigneur George Druschezky' [title page] 'Del Sig: Giorgio Druschetzky' [on the parts]

22-02

MS   H:K (0/166) The folder says 'Nr. 33'

H:Bn (FM 4/2048)

Adagio–Allegro

Menuetto

Romance Andante

Menuetto Allegretto

Rondo Allegro

Serenade in E♭, 'Composée Par Seigneur George Druschezky' [title page] 'Del Sig: Giorgio Druschetzky' [on the parts]

22-02

MS   H:K (0/186) The folder says 'Nr. 43'

H:Bn (FM 4/2068)

Adagio

Menuetto

Adagio

Menuetto Allegretto

Andante con Variazioni

Rondo

Parthia in E♭, arr. Giovanni Wendt (1745–1809)
22-02
MS H:K (128) Folder says Nr. 25.
    H:Bn (FM 4/ 2010)
    Allegro
    Menuetto
    Alternativo
    Andante
    Alegretto

Fournier, Giuseppe (Classic Period composer)

(4) *Notturni*
11-02
MS Allgemeine Musikgesellschaft, Zurich (XII 320, a-c)

Gebel, A. Franz (German, 1787–1843)

Deux Harmonies, Op. 11
22-02
EP (Wien: Magasin de l'imprimere chimique I.R., Nr. 882)
    H:K (717/VIII
    Allegro
    Andante
    Rondo
    Allegro
    Adagio
    Allegro

Gleissner, Franz (German, 1759–1818)

Journal d'harmonie
42-02
EP [no shelf-mark]
    G:BÜu [no shelf-mark]

Guglielmo, Pietro (Italian, 1728–1804)

Ouverture for 6 winds
G:BÜu (G-Ug-41)

Häusler, Ernesto (German, 1761–1837)

Tre Notturni, Op. 23
2-02
EP   (Offenbach: André, Nr. 2019)
   H:K (1037/IX)

Haydn, Joseph (Austrian composer, 1732–1809)

II Marsches
22-12
EP   (Leipzig: Kühnel, Nr. 489)
   H:K (726/VIII)

Marsch Nr. 1 / Clar. 1

Marsch Nr. 2

Holzinger, ? (early nineteenth century composer)

Die Belagerung und Eroberung Allessandria auf Türkische Musik
2221-12, piccolo Tambour, Grand tambour
MS H:K (1156/IX)

Die Belagerung und Eroberung Mantoua auf Türkische Musik
2221-12, piccolo, Piccolo & Grande Tambouro
MS H:K (1157/IX)

Kreith, Carlo (Austrian composer, d. 1809)

VI Original Ungarische Tänze für II Flöten, 6 works for 2 flutes
MS H:K (631/VIII)
MP Freiburg: Blasmusikverlag Schulz, Nr. 1101, 1992)

Deux Marsches in B♭, Op. 95
222-02
EP   (Wien: Josephe Eder, Nr. 452)
   H:K (666/VIII)

Clar. 1

Marcia per I morti, Op. 52

222-02

EP (Wien: Joseph Eder, Nr. 177)

H:K (660/VIII)

Partitta in B♭

222-02

EP (Wien, sul Graben: Giuseppe Eder, Nr. 425, ca. 1806)

H:K (656-657)

Allegro non troppo

Menuetto vivace

Adagio

Finale Allegretto

Partitta in B♭, Op. 57

22-02

EP (Wien: Giuseppe Eder, Nr. 199)

H:K (663/VIII)

Allegro

Menuetto

Andante Siclliano

Allegretto

Partitta in B♭, Op. 58

22-02

EP (Wien: Giuseppe Eder, Nr. 202)

H:K (663a)

Allegro non Troppo

Menuetto

Adagio

Allegretto

Partitta in D, Op. 59
21-02
EP   (Wien: Giuseppe Eder, Nr. 203)
      H:K (665/VIII)
      Allegro Brillante
      Menuetto Allegretto
      Allegretto Grazioso
      Andante
      Rondo

Partitta in E♭, Op. 63
21-02
EP   (Wien: Giuseppe Eder, Nr. 201)
      H:K (664/VIII)
      Allegro
      Menuetto Presto
      Adagio
      Finale

March, *Für das neu errichtete Wiener ScharfschützenKorps, Seiner Durchlaut dem in Nieder- und
Vorder-Oesterreich Commandierenden Herrn Generalen F.Z.M. Herzogen Ferdinand von Wür-
temberg mit tiefsten Ehrfurcht gewidmet und gnädigst angenohmen. Verfasset von Carl Kreith.*
222-32, piccolo, Grosse Trommel, 1 Tsamt Czinellen, 1 Kleine Trommel
EP   (Wien, am Graben: Josef Eder, Nr. 122)
      H:K (659)

Krommer, Franz (1759–1831, court composer in Vienna)

Allegro vivace pour 9 insts. [an early copy of Op. 73]
MS F:Pn (6579)

XIII Pièces pour deux clarinettes et viola
EP   F:Pn (LA.34.547)

Harmonie, Op. 67, Composée et dediéea Son Altesse Imp. et Roy Monseigneur l'Archiduc Joseph
Prince royale d'Hongrie et des Boheme, Palatin et Gouverneur Royale de royaume d'Hongarie
etc. etc.

222-02, contrabassoon

EP   (Wien, sur le Graben: Au Magasin de l'imprimerie chimique J. Reprio, Nr. 775)
H:K (2010)
Allegro Vivace
Adagio
Menuetto Allegretto
Allegro

Harmonie, Op. 69, Composée et dediée a Son Altesse Imp. et Roy Monseigneur l'Archiduc Joseph
Prince royale d'Hongrie et des Boheme, Palatin et Gouverneur Royale de royaume d'Hongarie
etc. etc.

222-02, contrabassoon

EP   (Wien, sur le Graben: Au Magasin de l'imprimerie chimique J. Reprio, Nr. 877)
H:K (2021)
Allegro
Andante Cantabile
Menuetto Allegretto
Rondo Allegretto

Partita, Op. 45, Nr. 2, for 222-02, contra, Trompette ad libitum

222-02, contrabassoon, Trompette ad libitum

EP   (Vienne, Kohlmarkt Nr. 269: Bureau d'Arts et d'Industrie Rue, Nr. 135)
H:K (2012)
Allegro
Romance Allegretto
Menuetto
Rondo

Partitta

222-02, contrabassoon

EP   (Wien: Ignazio Sauer)
H:K (700/VIII) the cover is marked 'Nr. 3'
Allegro Vivace
Andante Allegretto
Menuetto
Rondo

Six Marches, Op. 31

222-12, contrabassoon

EP   (Vienne, Rue Kohlmarkt: Bureau d'Arts et d'Industrie, Nr. 175)

H:K (2009) This publication is found in several libraries in Europe and was later republished by André in Offenbach as Plate Nr. 3135.

Nr. 1 Marche du Regiment Erz Herzog Carl

Nr. 2 Marche du Regiment Deutschmeister

Nr. 3

Nr. 4 Marche du Regiment Erz Carl

Nr. 5 Marche du Regiment Fürst Auersperg

Nr. 6

Kühn, ?

Carousel Rondo, nebst einem Carousel Ruf für die Trompete

221-02, contrabassoon

MS   H:K (760/VIII)

Kühnau, Johann (German composer, 1735–1805)

Pfingst. Motetta, Psalm 84

SATB, organ, 201-01

MS   F:Pn (MS. 2111 [1]), an autograph score (Feb. 12, 1766)

Lickl, Johann Georg (Austrian, 1769–1843)

Casation

III-01

EP   (Vienne: Joseph Eder au Magazine de Musique chez, Nr. 55)

H:K (756/VIII)

Adagio Cassazione

Menuetto Allegretto

Adagio

Polonese

Finale Presto

Quintetto
21-02
EP (Vienna: Magasino della Caes. Real. Priv. Stamperia chimica, Nr. 22)
H:K (757?VIII)
Adagio non molto
Romanze Adagio
Menuetto Allegretto
Rondo Allegretto

Maschek, Vincenc (Bohemian composer, 1755–1831)

Serenata in E♭
222-02
MS H:K (767/VIII)

Mattei, Stanislao (1750–1825)

Due Responsori (1784)
TTB, flute, viola, organ
MS I:Bsf (II-10) autograph score

Ridicolo ('*Esguito dal Sig. N.N. che peril numerosi anni era ridotto ad esser privo poco meno di tutti I denti*')
Solo bsn and strings
MS I:Bsf (XXII-7)

Miksichowsky, Antoni (Classical Period composer)

Partie
MS 201-02
S:L (Engelhart Nr. 194)

Mozart, Wolfgang Amadeus (Austrian composer, 1756–1791)

Deux Pieces d'Harmonie
222-02
EP (Leipsic: Breitkopf & Härtel, Nr. 65)
These are K.C.17.02 and K.C.1703
H:K (1019/IX)
Allegro
Menuetto

Adagio
Menuetto
Finale
Adagio
Menuetto
Romance Andante
Menuetto
Finale

Palladino, Giuseppe (Italian, eighteenth century composer)

Deus exaudi (1747)
SSBB, flutes, organ
MS I:Bsf (Ms. 51)

Pechatschek, Franz (Austrian, 1795–1840)

3 Bürger-Märche
222-22
EP (Vienne: der K.K. priv. chemische Druckerey, Nr. 91)
    H:K (1051/IX)

Pfeiffer, Francoise

VI Duos pour deux Cors
EP (Presbourg: Schauff)
    H:K (100)

Righini, Vincenzo (Italian, 1756–1812)

Serenade
22-02
EP Leipzig: Schmeidt & Rau
    S:L (Wenster Ö, Nr. 5)
    This is a three-movement work apparently taken from the larger *Armonia* (1797) for
    nine winds found in D:B (Ms. Mus. 337)

Serenata
22-02
EP (Leipsic: Schmiedt & Rau, Nr. 9)
    H:K (1024/IX)
    Larghetto
    Allegro vivace
    Menuetto
    Andante non troppo con (6) Variationen

Rohde, Michael (Classical Period composer)

Pfingst Stücke
Bass, 201-02, organ
MS   S:L (Wenster F, Nr. 22)

Salieri, Antonio (Italian composer in Vienna, 1750–1825)

Quintetto
201-02
MS   (autograph score) F:Pn (W.8.97)

Schiedermayr, Johann Baptist (German composer, 1779–1840)

VIII neue türkische Stücke, Op. 2
222-22, piccolo, contrabasson, percussion
EP   (Linz: Bürgl. Noten und Kupferdruckery)
  H:K (681/VIII) A note says these works can be performed as well by 22-12, piccolo
  Parade Marsch
  Feuer Marsch
  Allegretto quasi Allamande
  Allegro ma non tanto
  Allemande
  Rondo alla Marcia
  Polonese
  Pas Doubles Finale

Schnabel, Joseph Ignaz (1767–1831)

Missa quadragesimalis
SATB, organ, 2-033, corni di bassetti
EP   (Leuchart)
  F:Pn (D.13.850) score; (L.20190) parts

Schroeter, John Samuel (1752–1788)

(6) *Sonatas* for flute and cimbalo
  I:Bsf (M.S. 1-14)

Schwenke, Christian Friedrich Gottlieb (German composer, 1767–1822)

Marches & Danses
2022-02, Trompete ad Lib.
EP   (Hambourg: J. A. Böhme)
  H:K (2188)

Stadler, Giuseppe (di Praga) (Austrian composer, eighteenth century)

Due Marcie
1222-12, perc
EP   (Vienna: Magasino della Caes. Real. Priv. Stamperia chymica, Nr. 108)
    H:K (2022)

Stückel, Ferdinand

Partita turco
2022-22, piccolo, percussion
MS   H:K (1134/IX)
    Allegro Moderato
    Andante con molto – Siciliano
    Menuetto Allegro
    Allegro moderato
    Moderato
    Rondo
    Andante
    Rondo

Szekeressy, Antal (Hungarian, early nineteenth century composer)

VI Fanfares hongroises pour huit Trompettes
MS   H:K (2058), with incomplete parts
    Moderato
    Andante Maestoso
    Tempo di Marcia
    Andante
    Tempo risoluto
    Grave

Tomaschino

Marcia in D Major
2122-02
MS   S:L (Wenster I, Nr. 28)

Weber, Carl Maria von (German composer, 1786–1826)

Deux morceaux, for 22-02
Rondo (Ludwigsburg, 1818)
Adagio in F (July 6, 1808)
MS   (autograph score) F:Pn (MS. 408)

Reliquienschein des Meisters
EP   (Berlin: Morawe & Scheffelt, 1927). Weber works in this collection are,
   Nr. 11   *Kleiner Tusch* for 20 trumpets
   Nr. 32 *Walzer*, for 1022-12 [here in pf score]
   Nr. 49/6 Scene II, *Heinrich IV* for 21-02 [here in pf score]
   F:Pn (A.320)

Weber, Bernhard Anselm (German composer, 1766–1821)

Die Weihe der Kraft, [Music for a Stage Play]
222-02
MS H:K (2054)
   1. *Choral Ein feste Burg ist unser Gott* (composed by Dr. Martin Luther in Coburg, 1530)
   2. *Unmittelbar darauf der folgende Chor der Bergleute welche in Schacht arbeitin*
   3. *Chor der Nonnen*
   4. *Chor der Studenten*
   5. *Theresiens Sehnsucht*
   6. *Theresiens Todtenamt*
   7. *Marsch*
   8. *Duet in Wald*
   9. *Trauer Chor*
   10. *Krönungs-Marsch aus dem Schauspiel die Jungfrau von Orleans*

Winter, Peter von (Austrian composer, 1754–1825)

Partita
222-02
EP   (Wien: Bureau d'Arts et d'Industrie, Nr. 269)
   H:K (1129/IX)
   Molto Adagio
   Allegretto
   Allegro

ARRANGEMENTS

Anonymous

Acht Märsche für Turckische Musick, Volume I, containing marches by Kozeluch, Raffael, Vanhall, Beethoven, Krommer and Lipawsky
2022-11, serpent, perc
EP   (Offenbach, Nr. 1822)
     H:K (731/VIII)

Acht Märsche für Turckische Musick, Volume 2, for 2022-11, serpent, perc
EP   (Offenbach, Nr. 1816)
     H:K (731/2)

Marche de Bounaparte, á son entrée en Mantoue
22-02
EP   (Hambourg: Meyn)
     H:K (2179)

Sieben Märsche für Türkische Musick von verschiedenen Komponisten, Volume 3
2022-11, serpent, perc.
EP   (Offenbach: André, Nr. 1840)
     H:K (731/3)

Catel, Charles Simon (French, 1773–1830, as arr. ?)

Semiramis (opera)
222-02
MS   [Overture and 12 arias]
     H: K (1175/IX)

Cherubini, Luigi (Italian, 1760–1842)

Faniska (ballet), arr. Wenzel Sedlak
222-02, contrabassoon, 2 trumpets
MS   Brno Museum Library [cited by JH]
     This copy consists of 12 movements, called Sedlak's fortieth work.

Die Tage der Gefahr (opera)
222-02
MS   [Overture and 9 arias]
     H:K (1181/IX)

Die Tage der Gefahr nach Les Deux Journees
222-02, continuo
EP [Overture and 9 arias] Wien: Sauers Kunsthandlung, Handschrift
   H:K (1189/IX)

Lodoiska (opera)
222-02, contrabsn.
MS [Overture and 5 arias, 'Wien'], on the folder, '118'
   H:K (2056)

Cimarosa, Domenico (1749–1801)

Orazi e Curiazi (opera, 1797), arr. by the composer [!]
222-02
MS Esterházy Palace Library, Eissenstdt [cited by JH]
   This copy conisists of 9 movements.

Druschezky, Georg (as arr.)

42 Arien aus verschidenen Opern, 'Von Herrn Georg Druschezky Compositeur bey deiner
   Eminentz und Primas in Ungarn Graff Joseph Battiany'
22-02
MS H:K (0/117) The folder says 'Nr. 98'
   H:Bn (FM 4/1999)
   1. Müller, Sinfonia Allegro
   2. *wie ist mir zu muth*, Allegretto
   3. *Unbeststständig wie Wind*, Allegretto
   4. *Weiber womir mit disstren Blick*, Allegretto
   5. *Vater Liebe, Vater Schmerz*, Largo
   6. *Schwermut und Grillen*, Allegretto
   7. Finale, Allegro
   8. *Chor Von den Braminen*, Larghetto
   9. *Mit diesem Schleÿer Entreiss dich auf Ewig*, Adagio
   10. *Die Katze last das Mäuschen nicht*, Allegro
   11. *Noch ist sie nicht Verblüht*, Adagio
   12. *Gruss dem zweÿ Schwestern Von Prag*, Sinfonia Allegro
   13. *Ich bin der Schneider Katz, Katz, Katz*, Moderato
   14. *Wer niemals eingesperrt gewessen*, Allegretto
   15. *Gruss dem Neuen Sontags Kind*, Sinfonia Allegro
   16. Wegen meiner mach Dir Fräula die Sache imer fein, Allegro Moderato
   17. *Wer niemals einen Rausch hat gehabt*, Allegretto
   18. Rigini, *Ein Contro in Aspettato*, Sinfonia Allegro

19. *Sposa Sonia*, Larghetto
20. *Naumann in Dresden, Du Lebest Cora*, Andante espressivo
21. *Darf ich nicht zu Klagen*
22. Allegretto Rondo
23. *wie ein Hirt mein Volck*, Andante
24. *Trost und Freude, Prest Coro*
25. *Wonnezeit glänzt mir entgegen*, Larghetto amoroso
26. Allegro
27. *Zuerst nur ein Gott must kommen*, Andante
28. Müller, *Kaspar der Fagottist* in Bb, Sinfonia
29. Allegretto
30. Allegretto
31. Adagio
32. Andante molto
33. Allegretto
34. Allegro
35. Andantino
36. Allegro
37. Adagio
38. Allegretto
39. Allegro
40. Allegretto
41. Allegretto
42. Allegro

Divertissiment. Sur Differentes Pieces, arr. Georg Druschetzky
22-02
MS H:K (0/116) The folder says 'Nr. III'
    H:Bn (FM 4/1998)
    1. Marche
    2. Marche
    3. Marche
    4. Marche
    5. Marche
    6. Marche
    7. Englese
    8. Englese
    9. Polonesse
    10. A la Strassbourg
    11. Allegro
    12. Presto

13. La Chasse, Allegro
14. La Chasse, Allegro
15. Andante con (6) Variazione
16. Salieri, *Spiegel Arie, aus Semire und Azor*, Andante molto
17. Miller [Müller, Wenzel], *Schwermuth und Grillen aus dem Soramerfest der Braminen*, Allegretto
18. Miller [Müller, Wenzel], *Noch ist sie nicht verphlüt, aus dem Sommerfest der Mraminen*, Adagio
19. Rigini, Sposa Sonia, Larghetto
20. Allegro
21. romance
22. Süsmaÿer, *Aus dem Spiegel von Arcadien*, Allegro
23. *Aus dem Spiegel von Arcadien*, Andante
24. Miller [Müller, Wenzel], *Aus dem Fasgotist* [*Kaspar der Fagottist*], Allegro
25. Grand Polonesse con (6) Variationi
26. Adagio
27. La Russia, Allegro moderato
28. Vivace con (5) Variazioni
29. Adagio
30. Allegretto
31. Englese
32. Englese
33. Polonesse
34. *Wirbel Tanz der Fourlaner*, Moderato
35. Andantino
36. Allegretto
37. Andante
38. Ala Malburg, Allegretto
39. Haÿdn, *Andante con (2) Variazioni*
40. Andante
41. Adagio
42. Polonesse
43. Ballarina, Adagio
44. Moderato
45. Harlekino, Allegro
46. *Die Jäger*, Andantino
47. *Das Schwerdt schmieden*, Allegro
48. Adagio
49. Andante
50. Marche
51. Allegretto
52. Adagio, Moderato con (5) Variazioni
53. *Alla Majen*, Presto

54. Allegretto
55. Presto
56. Allegro
57. Andante
58. Larghetto
59. *Ariette sur le Tombeau*, Largo
60. Venturini, *Variation sur le Menuet* danse par Mademeiselle Venturini a Vienne,
    Thema und (5) Variazioni
61. *La Marche pour la Serenade*
62. *Der Todten*, March, adagio

'Priester Marsch aus der Oper Zauber-Flöte,' (Mozart) arr. Druschetzky
22-02
MS This arrangement is found on the back sides of the parts for Druschetzky's *Partie* in E♭
    for 22-02.
MS H:K (o/150) The folder says 'Nr. 18'
    H:Bn (FM 4/2032)

Opera Zauber-Flöte von W. Mozard
222-02
MS H:K (o.124) The folder says 'Nr. 105'
    H:Bn (FM4/2006)
    This arrangement consists of 18 arias.

Miserere a quatre Voce, et Organo
SATB, organ, 22-02
MS H:K (o/125)
    H:Bn (FM 4/2007)
    The original work is by Johann Philipp Kirnberger, 1721-1783, arr. here in
    16 movements.

Gallenberg, Wenzel Robert, von

Triumph-Marsch aus dem Ballet Alfred der Grosse, arr. Hieronymus Payer
Türkische Musick, or 43-742, piccolo, percussion
EP (Wien: Maketti, Handschrift, Nr. 1221)
    H:K (2044)

Grétry, André

Raul der Blaubart (opera), arr. Fischer, ?
222-02
MS H:K (697/VIII)

This copy consists of 12 arias. The Brno Museum Library, as cited by JH, has a manuscript arrangement called *Ballet Blubart*, arranged by Sedlak for 222-02, contrabassoon and 2 trumpets., which has been cataloged as being by Rossini. I believe the determination of the composer needs further study.

Pièces d'harmonie [arr. of the overture and arias of Grétry's *Panurge*, arr. Étienne Ozi]
6 winds
MS F:Pn (H2. 175)

Gyrowetz, Adalbert (Austrian, 1763–1850)

Die Hochzeit der Thetis und des Peleus, arr. Sedlak, *Eter Jahrgang*, No. 3.
222-02, contrabassoon, 2 trumpets
MS Brno Museum Library [cited by JH] Four different copyists names appear in the parts, suggesting that perhaps the players themselves had to make copies of this arrangement. Sedlak is called, *Kapelmeister der Durchlaucht des regierenden Fürsten pont und zu Lichtenstein.*

Agnes Sorel
222-02, contrabassoon
MS H:K (1173/IX)
This arrangement consists of the overture and 12 arias.

Haydn, Joseph

String Quartets, arr. by Nicolas Schmitt (b. 1779)
Premiere Suite
22-02
MS F:Pn (D.15.896)

5e Suite
22-02
MS F:Pn (L.1158, 1-6)

6e Suite
22-02
MS F:Pn (D.15.891)

Hummel, Johann Nepomuk

Helene e Paris (ballet), arr. Sedlak
222-02, contrabassoon
MS Esterházy Palace Library, Eisenstadt [cited by JH]
This arrangement consists of the overture and 12 arias.

Kinzi, Heinrich, arr. (Directeur de musique au deuxiéme Regiment Markgraf Guilleaume)

Piéces d'harmonie choisise des Opera les plus agreeable, tréshumblement dedié. A Son Altesse Royale Madame la Deuchesse douaariére Stephani Louise Adrienne
1042-02
MS H:K (2755) 8 movements

Müller, Wenzel

Das Neue Sonntagskind, (opera), arr. Giuseppe Haydenreich
22-02
MS H:K (121) Overture and 12 arias
   H:Bn (FM 4/2003)

Nicolo

Du Médicin Turc, (opera) Overture, arr. Amand Vanderhagen (Belgian clarinetist, 1753–1822)
2022-101, serpent ad lib.
EP   (Zuric: Jean George Naigueli, Nr. 262)
   H:K (977/VIII)

Ozi, Étienne (French bassoonist, as arr.)

Nr. 6 Nouvelle suite de piées d'harmonie [arr. of music of Gretry, Sacchini & Champein]
EP   Paris: Boyer]
   F:Pn (D. 16233)

Paer, Ferdinand (Italian, 1771–1839)

Sargines
222-02
MS H:K (866/VIII)
   This arrangement consists of 9 movements.

Griselda (opera), arr. C. Ahl
21-02
EP   [Part I, 6 movements] André Jean in Offenbach, Nr. 2226
   H:K (677/VIIIa)
   [Part II, 6 movements] André, Jean, Nr. 2227
   H:K (667/VIIIb)

Paisello, Giovanni (Italian, 1740–1816)

[unidentified] Opera, arr. for 6 winds
MS G: BÜu (P-Ai-39)

Il Re Theodoro in Venezia, (opera), arr. Guering, ?
22-02
MS   H:K (119) Overture and 23 arias, folder says 'Nr. 115'
     H:BN (FM 4/2001)

Payer, Hieronymus (nineteenth century)

Eichenkränze, Rondo Andante
1033-622, percussion
EP   (Wien im Michaelerhaus der k.k. Reitschule, Nr. 703)
     H:K (1191a)
     On the backside of these parts are the parts for a *Marsch* by the same composer.

Persuis, Louis–Luc Loiseau de (1769–1819)

Nina (ballet, 1813), arr. Sedlak
222-02, contrabassoon
MS   Melk Monastery, (V 567), cited by JH

Pleyel, Ignaz (Austrian, 1757–1831)

[15] *Pieces d'Harmonie pour Musique torque par divers Compositeur*
2022-22, serpent, perc.
EP   (Offenbach: André, Nr. 1836)
     H:K (1052/IX) 5 of the works are by Pleyel

Rossini

Tancredi, arr. Sedlak
222-02
MS   Brno Museum Library [cited by JH]
     This copy belonged to the Chor Augustine Library, Stare Brno.

Wilhelm Tell, arr. Sedlak(?)
222-02, contrabassoon, 2 trumpets, trombone
MS   Brno Museum Library [cited by JH]
     Sedlak's name does not appear; only various copyists dated 1831.

Soller, Antonio (1729–1783, as arr.)

Suite d'harmonie tirées des opera et operas comiques
22-02
EP   (Paris: Sieber), in 5 volumes
     F:Pn (L.19914)
     This print includes an arrangement for 22-02 of Haydn's *Symphony*, Hob. I, 51.

Steibelt, Daniel (arr. Carl Andreas Göpfert)

Combat Naval
222-12, serpent and grand Tambour ad lib.
EP   (Bonn: Simrock, Nr. 346)
    H:K (2048)

Stumpf, Johann Christian (German, d. 1801, as arr.)

Grande Serenade tirées des oeuvres de Mozart
22-02
EP   (Hambourg: chés les fréres Meyn, Nr. 13)
    H:K (922/VIII)
    Allegro molto
    Andante
    Allegro

Devienne, *Les Visitandines* (opera)
22-02
EP   [6 arias] Hambourg: Böhmel, Jean August
    H:k (923/VIII)

Winter, P., *Das unterbrochene*, (opera), *Pieces d'harmonie*, Part 3
22-02
EP   (Offenbach: André, Nr. 1204), 5 movements
    H:K (1195 koll. 3)

Winter, *Das unterbrochene*, (opera), *Pieces d'harmonie*, Part 4
22-02
EP   (Offenbach: André, Nr. 1205), 6 movements
    H:K (1195 koll. 4)

Martin, *Capricciosa*, (opera), *Pieces d'harmonie*, Part 5
22-02
EP   (Offenbach: André, Nr. 1359), 6 movements
    H:K (1195 koll. 5)

Paër, *la Camilla*, (opera), *Pieces d'harmonie*, Part 6
22-02
EP   (Offenbach: André, Nr. 1366), 6 movements
    H:K (1195 koll. 6)

Paër, *la Camilla*, (opera), *Pieces d'harmonie*, Part 7
22-02
EP   (Offenbach: André, Nr. 1367), 6 movements
    H:K (1195 koll. 7)

Paër, *Il morto vivo*, (opera), *Pieces d'harmonie*, Part 8
22-02
EP (Offenbach: André, Nr. 1578), 6 movements
    H:K (1195 koll. 8)

Vogel, Johann Christoph (1756–1788)

Overture de Démophon, arr. unknown
222-12, serpent, or 22-02
EP (Leipzig: Kühnel, Nr. 408)
    H:K (683/VIII)

Weber, Carl Maria von

Der Freischütz, arr. Flachs, ?
2222-02
MS G: BÜu (W-Eb-35)

Weigl, Josef (Austrian, 1766–1846)

Die Uniform, arr. unknown
Harmonie for 222-02
MS H:K (884/VIII) Overture and 11 arias

Winter, Peter

Vologesus, (ballet), arr. unknown
22-02
MS H:K (1179/IX)
    This copy consists of an overture and 9 movements.

Supplementary Nineteenth–Century Repertoire

IN 1993 ON YET ANOTHER LONG VISIT to the music division of the National Library in Paris I not only found some particularly interesting band music which was not included in my earlier volumes, but also some interesting treatises which are included in the following.

Regarding the following original titles, 'Harmonie' now refers to the large nineteenth century band and not the *Harmoniemusik* of the eighteenth century. The term, *Air varié* in nineteenth century France band repertoire meant 'Theme and Variations.'

Altafulla, Ubaldo-Antonio (Italian, nineteenth century)

Mesal à tre voci
TTB e stramenti á fiato obbligati
MS I:Bsf (M.A. VII-13)

Anonymous

Eccosse
22-22, piccolo, posthorn, contrabassoon
MS Brno Museum Library [cited by JH]

(6) *Deutsche* Dances
42-42, piccolo, contrabassoon, tambora, grand tambor

Bellini, Vincenzo (Italian, 1801–1835), arr. Caruli, Benedetto (Italian, 1797–1877)

Bianca e Fernando, for 2032-12, clarino piccolo
MS I:Bsf (M.B. IV-10)

Debali, Francisco José (1791–1859)

Debali was a Hungarian band director who worked in Italy before moving to Montevideo, Paraguay. Between 1841–1848 he wrote the music for the national anthem of Paraguay. His manuscripts are in the Museo Histórico Nacional in Montevideo, for which the following shelf-marks pertain.

Armonia
band
MS (Inventario Nr. 1), score and parts

Armonia
band
MS (Inventario Nr. 2), parts

Partia o Armonia
band
MS (Inventario Nr. 3a), score

Introducción a un aria de Atila de Verdi, arr. for band
MS (Inventario Nr. 4a), score

La Batalla de Cagancha,
band
MS (Inventario Nr. 307), parts

Concerto per Corno e Obligato a Clarinetto
band
MS (Inventario Nr. 8a), score and parts

Divertimento para clarinete y banda
MS (Inventario Nr. 11), score

Divertimento per Tromba [Horn] y Chiavi
MS (Inventario Nr. 14a), score

(2) *Marcha*
band
MS (Inventario Nr. 14b, 14c), score and parts

Obligado para trompa [horn] y trompeta
band
MS (Inventario Nr. 22), score

(6) *Marcha*
MS (Inventario Nr. 25, 29, 33a, 33b, 33c, 33d), score

(4) *Marcha*
band
MS (Inventario Nr. 27, 31a, 34a, 34b), score and parts

Gran Marcha
band
(Inventario Nr. 28), score

Due Marcia per Musica Militaire
MS (Inventario Nr. 26), parts

Marcha
band
MS (Inventario Nr. 30), parts

Vals
band
MS (Inventario Nr. 31b), score and parts

Escocesa
band
MS (Inventario Nr. 31c), score and parts

Polonesa
band
MS (Inventario Nr. 31d), score and parts

Adagio
band
MS (Inventario Nr. 35b), score

Introducción y Mazurca
band
MS (Inventario Nr. 36), score and parts

(2) *Paso doble*
band
MS (Inventario Nr. 38a, 38b), score and parts

Credo
3 part voices and band
MS (Inventario Nr. 43) score and parts

Credo
3 voices and band
MS (Inventario Nr. 44), score

Credo
3 part voices and band
MS (Inventario Nr. 45), parts

Misa
3 part voices and band
MS (Inventario Nr. 68), score and parts

Misa para música military
3 part voices and band
MS (Inventario Nr. 70), score

Tantum Ergo
tenor, chorus and band
MS (Inventario Nr. 125), score

Sinfonia
band
MS (Inventario Nr. 134), score

(2) *Sinfonia*
band
MS (Inventario Nr. 139, 140a), score and parts

Solo para Trompa [Horn] y Banda
MS (Inventario Nr. 143), score

(7) *Vals*
band
MS (Inventario Nr. 153, 155a, 155b, 156, 158, 159, 162), parts

Suonata per Musica Militaire
MS (Inventario Nr. 144), parts

Gran Vals Nr. 1
band
MS (Inventario Nr. 146), score and parts

Gran Vals
band
MS (Inventario Nr. 147), parts

Vals Nr. 3
band
MS (Inventario Nr. 150), score

(2) *Marcha*
band
MS (Inventario Nr. 155c, 155d), parts

Vals Nr. 4
band
MS (Inventario Nr. 157), score

Vals e Polonesa
band
MS (Inventario Nr. 160), parts

Gran Vals con Introducción
band
MS (Inventario Nr. 164b), score and parts

Variaciones para música military
band
MS (Inventario Nr. 168), score and parts

(2) *Himno Nacional Uruguayo*
band
MS (Inventario Nr. 177, 178), score

Marcha
band
MS (Inventario Nr. 258a), score

Divertimento para corno ingles y banda
MS (Inventario Nr. 279b), score and parts

Composizion
band
MS (Inventario Nr. 286b), score

Sinfonia
band
MS (Inventario Nr. 294), score

Gran Polonesa
band
MS (Inventario Nr. 392), parts

Ballabile
band
MS (Inventario Nr. 586b), score and parts

Andante y Polnesa
band
MS (Inventario Nr. 742i), parts

Media Cañ, Tabapi, Triste y Campana
band
MS (Inventario Nr. 37a), parts

Eder, Philipp

[Funeral march]
21-12
MS Melk Monastery Archive (Nr. 1724), ciited by JH
   This score is dated 30.6.1813 for the burial of P. Basilius Wagner. This score is in the
   hand of Georg Eggenberger.

Halévy, Jacques François (French, 1799–1862)

Marche heroïque, 'execute en translation de cendres de Napoleon, 25 Feb. 1842 [another hand
   writes 1841]. This is a major symphonic march marked 'Moderato comment e dolore,'
   performed when the remains of Napoleon arrived back in Paris.
large band with no saxophones
MS F:Pn (L. 18347) Parts only, including one ophicleide part, in 13 copies!

Hammer, Richard (second half, nineteenth century)

Marche funèbre, Op. 35
harmonie militaire
MS F:Pn (9883/3) Autograph score

Herrfurth, M.

[Untitled work]
121-11
MS Melk Monastery Archive (Nr. 1723), cited by JH

Jokl, Josef

Marsch Nr. 2
Brass
MS Melk Monastery Archive (Nr. 2874), cited by JH

Kling, Hippolyte (French, 1842–1918)

Souvenir de 1792! Poeme symphonique pour harmonie
EP   (Paris: l'Orphéon, 1881)
   F:Pn (K. 41401)

Klose, Hyacinthe (French, 1808–1880)

Duo, Op. 20, for oboe and clarinet
d'harmonie militaire or piano
MS F:Pn (K. 1702)

Polka des Princes
band
MS F:Pn (12137) autograph score, 1847

Kreutzer, Rolophe (German, 1766–1831)

Marche pour l'inauguration du Portrait du Roi dans la sale de Union des Artistes de sa musique, 1816,
2222-02
MS F:Pn (Cons. Collection) Autograph score
> This is a very nice concert march of about 100 bars by the same Kreutzer for whom Beethoven named his famous Sonata.

Landa, W. (nineteenth century Kapellmeister, Kaiser Franz Josef Infantrie Reg. N.1.)

Giuramento-Marsch
band
MS I:Bsf (M.L. 1-4)

Lenepvue, Charles (French, 1840–1910)

Hymne funébre et triumphal (text by Victor Hugo)
chorus and orchestra or band
MS F:Pn (MS 6791) Autograph score

Ode Triomphale à Jeanne d'Arc (1897)
chorus and orchestra, followed by a version for band
MS F:Pn (MS 6913)

Leprevost, Alexandre (nineteenth century French organist)

Halte dans les bois
TTBB chorus, saxhorn contralto in B♭, saxotromba alto in E♭, saxotromba baritone in B♭,
    saxhorn basse in B♭, saxhorn contrebasse in B♭ and timpani
EP   Published in Paris by Adolphe Sax
    F:Pn (Cons. D. 6989)

Meyerbeer, Giacomo (German composer, 1791–1864)

Der Bayereische Schützen-Marsch
male choir and large brass ensemble
MS F:Pn (MS.11.288) Autograph score

Kronungs-Marsch, dedicated to Wilhelm I
orchestra and band
EP   (Berlin: Schlesinger)
    F:Pn (D.8420)
    > This is for a large band, based on the Sax system, which is independent and does not double the orchestra

Fackeltanz
Band
MS F:Pn (MS.11.289) Autograph score, 'Berlin 15 May, 1853'

Fackeltanz, Nr. 3, '*Arrangée pour musique militaire du Systime Sax*,' by J. Mohr
Band
EP   (Paris: Brandus, 1854)
     F:Pn (D. 8426); (Cons. L. 795), another copy

Fackeltänze, full scores for military band arranged by Wieprecht
band
EP   (Berlin: Bote & Bock)
     F:Pn [D.8425 (1-4)]
     1. B-dur, 29 pages
     2. Eb-dur, 33 pages
     3. C-moll, 84 pages
     4. C-dur, 47 pages

Mohr, Jean-Baptiste-Victor (French, 1823–1891)

Air Varié
cornet and orchestra d'harmonie, or piano
EP   (Paris: Lafleur, 1867)
     F:Pn (K.35664) Piano only

(8) *Morceau pour musique d'Infantrie et cavalerie*
band(s)
MS F:Pn [D. 4336 (16)]
     This is 7 volumes of waltzes, polkas, etc., and Nr. 7 is an *Air Varié* for solo Eb clarinet.

Quatour
SATB saxophones
EP   (Paris: A. Sax, 1864)
     F:Pn (K.10.242) This library also contains many etudes for winds, mostly for horn,
     by Mohr.

Moliter, S.

(12) *Deutch tänze*
3122-02, organ, timpani
MS Melk Monastery Archive (Nr. 1806), cited by JH

Momigny, Lysias de (Belgian, nineteenth century)

Te Deum, Op. 137
SAATB chorus and band
EP   (Paris: Chez Tournier, 1854)
    F:Pn (D.8.439)
      1. Te Deum, Allegro pompose
      2. Sanctus
      3. Te per Orbem (for a smaller ensemble)
      4. Te Rex Glorie
      5. Judex Crederis
      6. Saluum Fac Populum Tuumpomine
      7. Et non confondar in aeternum Amen

Mozart, arr. Amand Polster ['Zur Messe']

Priestermarsch from *The Magic Flute*
220-02, organ
MS   Melk Monastery Archive (Nr. 1695), cited by JH

Muller, Georges (German, 1805–1898)

Marche pour orchestra militaire
MS   F:Pn (L. 2799)

Munch, Charles (French, nineteenth century)

Overture à grande harmonie
1222-122, serpent
MS   F:Pn (MS.14.220) An early nineteenth century original work
MP   www.whitwellbooks.com
    Largo-Allegro
    Andante poco Adagio
    Minuet & Trio

Päer, Ferdinand (Italian, 1771–1839)

Marriage de Napoleon Ier avec l'Archiduchessse Marie Louise d'Autriche, Quatre grandes Marches pour musique militaire. April 1, 1810
MS   F:Pn [D. 9161 (1-4)]
MP   www.whitwellbooks.com
    Nr. 1, 10-page score
    Nr. 2, 8-page score

Nr. 3, 16-page score
Nr. 4, 13-page score
Päer adds a note informing us that these marches were played in the gallery of the museum at the moment Their Majesties were passing.

Pierne, Gabriel (French, 1863–1937)

Marche solenelle pour militaire harmonie (Concours de l'Exposition, 1888)
Large band
MS F:Pn (MS.5614)
This is an outstanding symphonic march in a 24 page score for large band with saxophones.

Pastorale varée dans le style ancient
1112-11
EP (Paris: Durand, 1898)
F:Pn (D.9822)

Quintet, for winds
EP (Paris: Leduc, 1887)
F:Pn (D.9835)

Polster, Amand

[Untitled funeral work]
SATB, 22-223
MS Melk Monastery Archive (Nr. 1877), cited by JH

Ramain, J. (French, nineteenth century)

Air Varié for Ophicleide and orchestra d'harmonie
EP (Paris: Lafleur, 1867) a publication of 24 separate parts
F:Pn (K. 1902)

Reali, ? (Italian, Maestro del concerto di Porto S. Giorgio)

Kyrie
TTB chorus, clarino, organ
MS I:Bsf (FC.F.I.8)

Resch, Paul

Overture (autograph score, dated April 25, 1812)
222-02
MS Melk Monastery Archive (Nr. 2781), cited by JH

Reicha, Anton (Bohemian, 1770–1836)

Harmonie complete ou Symphonie sans insts. à cordes ('Symphony without strings') This is
the autograph score of the famous *Commemoration Symphony*, or *Symphony* for 3 bands
by Reicha.
MS F:Pn (L.19656), Autograph presentation score
MP www.whitwellbooks.com
The score carries the note, *Cette Symphonie est Concertante. Les parties detachées de la
musique en l'honneur de la Nation française. La partition de cetteSymphonie le trouve a la cata-
logue Nr. 1 Partition et il y a dans le meme volumes des Sceruirs d'harmonie.*

2 Andantes et un adagio
1011-, English horn
MS F:Pn (MS 12022)

Nr. 4 Grand Quintet, in E minor
woodwind quintet
MS F:Pn (MS 2506) Autograph score

Quintet in E♭
woodwind quintet
MS F:Pn (MS. 2507)

Quintet in A minor
woodwind quintet
MS F:Pn (MS. 2508)

24 Quintets, a manuscript copy which belonged to Dauprat, horn teacher at the
Paris Conservatory.
MS F:Pn [MS. L. 4503 (1-4)]

[First editions of the famous quintets]
6 Quintets, Op. 88
EP (Paris: Boieldieu, jeune)
    F:Pn (Ac.e.5.21)

6 Quintets, Op. 91
EP (Paris: Boieldieu, jeune)
    F:Pn (Ac.e.5.22)
    (Ac.e.5.134) another copy

6 Quintets, Op. 99
EP (Paris: Boieldieu, jeune)
    F:Pn (Ac.e.5.23)

6 Quintets, Op. 100
EP   (Paris: Zetter)
     F:Pn (Ac.e.5.24)

'*Sur la musique comme art purement sentimental, avec des remarques philosophiques et critiques sur les operations morales de notre être.* An autograph treatise by Reicha.
MS F:Pn (Res.F.1646)

Rossini, Gioacchino (Italian, 1792–1868)

Andante e tema con variazione
1011-01
MS F:Pn (Conservatory collection) Autograph score

Trio
11-01
MS F:Pn (L. 19748)

Le Rendez-vous de chasse
4 solo trumpets in D, 4 horns in D, 3 cornet à piston in A, 2 ripieno trumpets in D, 3 trombones, 'basses à vent,' timpani. At a later time, in different ink and style, he added optional string and woodwind parts for a bigger ending.
MS F:Pn (MS.2436) Autograph score

Sinfonie La Gazza Ladra, arr. for large band
MS Münster, Fürst zu Bentheimische Collection (R-os-117.1)

Overture to *Tancredi,* arr. F. Uth, 1852
2 flutes
MS Melk Monastery Archive (Nr.1025), cited JH

Roth, J. Cretien (French writer, nineteenth century)

'*Les musiques militaries in France,*' a 24 page article, ca. 1852
MS F:Pn (A.141)
     [Recueil 67 (4)], another copy?

Sax, Adolphe (Belgian inventor, 1814–1894)

'*De la necessite des musiques militaries,*' 15 pages
EP   (Paris: Librarie centrale, 1867)
     F:Pn [Recueil 117 (11)]

Schneider, Friedrich (German, 1786–1853)

Der 67ste Psalm, Op. 102
2 male choirs, winds, timpani, celli and string bass
EP   (Berlin: Trautwein, 1844)
  F:Pn (D.13.613)

Schneitzhoeffer, Jean-Madeleine (French, 1785–1852)

Symphonie Bataille, for a national 'monster concert,' held at the Pantheon in July, 1831.
Band and chorus
MS F:Pn (19985 A-J) one loose folder and 9 huge boxes of approximately 126 parts
  with doubling
  F:Pn (L.19986) more than 200 choral parts
  1. *Andante*
  2. *[no title]*
  3. *Drapeau*
  4. *Appel de Cavalerie*
  5. *Le drapeau*
  6. *La Charge*
    [no title]Canon
  7. *Courons a la vengeance*
  8. *Priere*
  9. *La charge*
  10. *La Generale*
  11. *Attague*
  [unnumbered] *La Marseillaise* (actually a longer original work based on the
  famous hymn)

Sor, Ferdinand (1778–1839)

Marche compose pour la musique militarie
MS F:Pn (A.48.040) Autograph score for piano, 4 hand

Sudre, Jean-François (French, nineteenth century violinist and inventor)

An extant collection describing Sudre's *la Téléphone* system of military trumpet signals,
  which developed into his Universal Language, and which finally developed into a system
  of communication for the deaf. For a full discussion see www.whitwellessays.com.
'Téléphone'
EP   (Paris: Impr. Royale, 1844)
  F:Pn [Recueil 150 (19)]

'*Language musicale …*'
EP   (Paris: Chez d'auteur)
　　F:Pn (40.B.624)
　　(L. 8642) Another copy

'*Repports sur la langue musicale inventée par M. F. Sudre*'
EP   F:Pn (80.B.2825) Press reviews from France, Belgium and England

'*Repport … au nom de la Commission chargée d'examiner de procede téléphonique …*'
EP   F:Pn [Recueil 234 (9)]

'*Rapports dur la langue Musicale*'
EP   F:Pn [Recueil 91 (8)]

Valenta, Bedrich (Bohemian, d. 1934)

Prostne dorostencu
piano and band
MS   A:Wn (Sm 22825), late nineteenth century

Wachs, Paul (Italian, nineteenth century)

Madrilena
band
MS   I:Bsf (FC.W.X.8)

Wagner, arr. ?

March from Tannhäuser
band
MS   I:Bsf (FC.W.X.89)

Wieprecht, Wilhelm (German composer and conductor, 1802–1872)

Deflier marsch, Links! Rechts!
military band
MS   F:Pn (MS.12456) Autograph score

Fanfare (Nr. 12 in *Musik am Preussischen Hofe* (Leipzig: 1897)
An attractive publication of a series of one Tusch and 5 Fanfares by Wieprecht and one by
　　Danckelmann, for large brass ensemble for the wedding of Prince Wilhelm and Princess
　　Augusta von Sachsen-Weimar in 1829. Each composition is prefaced by an explanation
　　of where in the day or ceremony it was used.
EP   F:Pn [Aa.20 (12)] Score

Wiss, H. B. (French, nineteenth century composer)

Messe Imperiale pour musique militaire dedicated to the victories of the army under Napoleon III.
band, a 'field mass,' a mass without singers
MS F:Pn (D.13.315)
1. [title cropped] … *rirouas*
2. *Gloria*
3. *Credo*
4. *Offertorium*
5. *Sanctus*
6. *Apres la consecration*
7. *Priere pour l'Empereur*

Witmann, G. (French, nineteenth century band conductor)

Collection of 60 *Sonneries et Fanfares de Chasse*
1 to 4 trumpets
EP (Paris: Evette & Schaefer, 1910)
F:Pn [L.9.653 (1-4)]

Collection of 64 *Marches pour trompettes de cavalerie, avec ad. lib. Percussion*
EP (Paris: Evette & Schaefer, 1911)
F:Pn (L.9.650)

Collection of 64 *Marches*
EP (Paris: Evette & Schaefer, 1914)
F:Pn (L.9.651)

Collection of 72 *Marches, retraites, etc.*
EP (Paris: Evette & Schaefer, 1914)
F:Pn (L.9.021)

Wittmann, J. B. (French, nineteenth century band conductor)

Grande fantasie (1863)
solo trombone and band
MS F: Pn (MS.7093) Autograph score
An easy band score, but a difficult solo part.

Zabala, Nicola (Italian, nineteenth century)

Missa
SSAT soli, SATB chorus, oboes, trumpets, continuo
MS I:Bsf (M.Z. 1-5)

Collections

Journal de Musique Militaire
42-12, piccolo, serpent, percussion
EP   (Lyon: Leyroy)
     Allgemeine Musikgesellschaft, Zurich (XIII 3074, a-L)
     37 early nineteenth century arrangements for band

Journal de Musique Militaire
2222-12, serpent or 42-12, piccolo, serpent, percussion
EP   (Lyon: Chanel)
     Allgemeine Musikgesellschaft, Zurich (XIII 3075, a-L)
     37 early nineteenth century arrangements for band

Early Twentieth-Century Repertoire
for Large Ensembles of Winds

WHEN I BEGAN WRITING the *History and Literature of the Wind Band and Wind Ensemble* some thirty years ago I made the decision to limit my research to that before the year 1900, because a number of band directors working in 1980 had a working knowledge of bands in the twentieth century. Nevertheless, over the years I accumulated a list of early twentieth century wind music which I found interesting. Many of the following listings are the result of my study years ago of two basic collections then available, the *Die Musik in Geschichte und Gegenwart* (Basel, 1958) and the fifth edition of the Grove, *Dictionary of Music* (New York, 1954). The entries I have taken from these two sources are identified by the respective symbols [MGG] and [G5].

In addition, I have kept track of compositions which have appeared in the publications of various publishers and these are indicated by the name of the publisher. Finally, although outside my main research focus, I have taken notice of a number of scores I found in various libraries in the course of my travels. These entries follow the R.I.S.M. *Sigla* (where one can, online, also find library mailing addresses), often together with the actual shelf-marks.

While this list is incomplete, for reasons given above, I believed it important to include this repertoire to demonstrate to the reader that throughout the twentieth century there has been a considerable interest among composers everywhere for writing serious repertoire for band. But it has been a world quite removed from the publishers of the commercial music used in music education, which unfortunately is all that many young band conductors have ever experienced.

It may be of particular interest to some readers to investigate the numerous interesting compositions listed here which were written in Germany during WWII. I am thinking here not of the programmatic or textual sense, but of the subjective insights the music might reveal.

Aeschfachter, Walther (Bern, Switzerland, b. 1901)

Suite (1943)
brass ensemble
MS [MGG]

Turnmusik, Nr. 1 & 2 (1949)
brass ensemble
MP (Adliswil: Ruh)

Praeludium super unum tonum (1949)
brass ensemble
MP (Adliswil: Ruh)

Alain, Jehan (French)

Invention (1937)
wind instruments
MS [G5]

Amirow, Fikret (Russian, b. 1922)

(5) *Stücke* (1953)
brass sextet
MS [MGG]

Amy, Gilbert (b. 1936 in Paris)

Alpha-Beth (1964)
6 winds
MS [MGG]

Apostel, Hans Erick (b. 1901 in Karlsruhe)

Intrada, Op. 23 (1954)
large brass ensemble with percussion
MP (Vienna: UE)

Festliche March
wind orchestra
MP (Vienna: Doblinger, 1962)

Bantock, Sir Granville (English, 1868–1946)

Hebrides poem, Tir Nan Og (1945)
wind orchestra
MS [MGG]

The Burden of Babylon, Praeludium & Motet (1927)
chorus, brass and percussion
MS [MGG]

Barber, Samuel (American, b. 1910)

A Stopwatch and an Ordnance Map (1940)
male voices, 4 horns, 3 trombones, tuba and timpani
MS [G5]

Barrows, John (American hornist, b. 1913)

(2) *Concert Marches* (1943, 1945)
military band
MS [G5]

March of the Gremblins (1944) for military band
MS [G5]

Bate, Stanley (English, b. 1913)

Pastorale, Op. 48a
military band
MS [G5]

Bauer, Marion (American, b. 1897)

Patterns (1946–1949)
10 winds
MS [G5]

Baussnern, Waldemar (1866–1931)

Wer weiss wo
baritone solo, male chorus, 2 trumpets, 2 horns, trombones, timpani
MP (Essen: Rheinischer Musikverlag)

Beck, Conrad (Swiss, b. 1901)

Der Tod des Oedipus, Cantata, 1928
solo voices, chorus, brass, percussion and organ

Beckerath, Alfred von (German, b. 1901)

Sinfonia for winds
MS [MGG]

Vld, Suite
wind orchestra
MS [MGG]

Gedächinemusik
wind orchestra
MS [MGG]

Heitere Suite
wind orchestra

Ein Bläsertag
large wind orchestra
MS [MGG]

Musik,
two wind orchestras
MS [MGG]

(4) *Intraden*
three brass choirs
MS [MGG]

Intrada
TB voices, 3 brass choirs
MS [MGG]

Bilderbuch
6 winds
MS [MGG]

Musica
male chorus and winds
MS [MGG]

Behred, Fritz (b. 1889, Berlin)

Oktett, Suite, Op. 116
1121-, bass clarinet
MS [MGG]

Benedikt, Walter (Austrian)

(2) *Marches*, ca. 1913
MS A:Wn (Sm 23354, 233550)

Bentzon, Niels (Danish, b. 1919)

Kammerkonzert, Op. 52 (1948)
3 pianos, winds and percussion
MS [Amsterdam: ISCM, 1949)

Berezovsky, Nicolay (b. 1900, Russia)

Suite, Op. 24 (1939)
7 brass
MS [G5]

Berger, Theodor (Austrian, b. 1905)

(4) *Serenades*
male chorus, winds and percussion
MS [MGG]

Bernier, René (Belgian, b. 1890)

Epitaphe II (1945)
wind orchestra
MS D:Mbs [a copy]

Biefeld, Karl (German, 1866–1944)

Jubiläumsmarsch
wind orchestra
MS [MGG]

Binet, Jean (Swiss, b. 1893)

Psalm XIII (1924)
male chorus and wind band
MS [G5]

Blum, Robert (German, b. 1900)

An Orpheus (1950)
13 winds
MS [MGG]

Bowles, Paul (American, b. 1910)

Concerto (1947) for piano, winds and percussion
[G5]

Breau, ?

Deutsches Turnerlied (1926)
unison chorus and brass
MS D:Mbs (Mus.Ms. 9357) Autograph score

Frankenlied (1928)
9 brass
MS D:Mbs (Mus.Ms. 9374), Autograph score

Brun, François

Invénales Fetes de la Jeanesse, in three movements
wind orchestra
MP (Leduc, 1969)
    D:Mbs (40 Mus.Pr. 46712) copy

Brunetti-Pasano, August (Austrian, b. ca. 1926)

De Profundis
8 brass
MS A:Sca (Hs. 1141)

Burkhard, Willy (Swiss b. 1900)

Incidental Music for Oedipus Rex, Op. 72 (1944)
spoken chorus, winds, percussion
MS [G5]

Bush, Alan (English, b. 1900)

Pavane for the Castleton Queen, Op. 42 (1935)
brass band
MS [G5]

Busser, Henri (French, b. 1872)

The following are the composer's transcriptions for wind band.
Divertissement Danse from *Les Noces Corinthiennes*
MP (Choudens)

Marche de Fete
MP (Durand)

Minerve Overture
MP (Buffet-Crampon)

Prelude to Les Noces
MP (Choudens)

Fantasie from *La Ronde des Saisons*
MP (Buffet-Crampon)

Búttner. Max (German, 1873–1956)

Marsch
wind orchestra
MS D:Mbs (Mus.Ms. 11023)

Rondach-Lied
15 winds
MS D:Mbs (Mus.Ms. 10900a)

6- & 8-part *tower music*
MS D:Mbs

Chapdevielle, Pierre (French, b. 1906)

Cantata de la France retrouvée (1946)
tenor, male chorus wind orchestra, percussion, harp, piano
MS [MGG]; [G5]

Caplet, André (French, 1878–1925)

Suite Persane
2222-02
MS [MGG]
> The first performance was given in Paris, March 9, 1901, by the *Société pour instruments à vent*.

Casadesus, François Louis (French, 1870–1945)

London Sketches
10 winds
MP (Deisz)

Casella, Alfredo (Italian, 1893–1947)

Introduzione, corale e marcia, Op. 57 (1935)
wind orchestra
MS [MGG]

Cellier, Alexandre-Eugene (French, b. 1883)

Paesiello, ed. Cellier, *Marche funébre pour la mort de general Hoch*
Band
MP (Paris: Leduc)

Cohn, Arthur (American, b. 1910)

Music for 4 Trumpets and 3 Trombones, Op. 9 (1933)
MS [G5]

Cooke, Arnold (English, b. 1906)

Suite (1931)
6 brass
MS [MGG]

Cools, Eugene (French, 1877–1936)

Marsch for the 109th Infanterie-Regiments band
MS [MGG]

Cossart, Leland (German, b. 1877)

Suite, Op. 19
2222-02
MS D:Bn (Nr. 73317)

Darthu, Paul

Le Rata
chorus and wind orchestra
MP (Paris: Laffe, 1913)
    F:Pn (K.20069) a copy

David, Carl Heinrich (Swiss, 1884–1951)

Suite
wind orchestra (1950)
MS [MGG, G5]

David, Johann Nepomuk (Austrian, b. 1895)

Introit, Chorale and Fugue on a Theme by Bruckner, Op. 25
organ and 9 winds
MS [G5]

Davies, Henry Walford (1869–1941)

Märsche for wind orchestra (1921, 1934–1939)
MS [MGG]

Demuth, Norman (English, b. 1938)

Concerto for Saxophone and Band (1938)
[G5]

The Sea (1939) for band
MS [G5]

Regimental March for the Royal Pioneer Corps (1943)
MS [G5]

Dietl, A. R. (Austrian)

Die Blumenteufel, a march (1915)
Band
MS A:Sc (Hs. 685)

Dorbe, Hans (German, associated with the theater in Munich)

Parademarsch (1907)
MS D:Mbs (Mus.Ms. St. Th. 1333) Autograph score

Dupré, Marcel (French, b. 1886)

Verdun, poeme heroique
organ and brass, Op. 33
MP (New York: Gray, 1936)

Effinger, Cecil (American, b. 1914)

(6) *Military Marches* (1942)
MS [G5]

Suite
band (1944)
MS [G5]

Chorale and Fugue (1949)
band
MS [G5]

Improvisation
clarinet and band (1950)
MS [G5]

Elgar, Edward (English, 1857–1934)

Severn Suite
brass band
MS GB:Lbm (add. 49974B) sketches

Erpf, Hermann (German, b. 1891)

Hymne Himmlische Ernte
chorus and winds
MS [MGG]

Fach, Adolf (German)

Marsch in E♭ (1903)
MS D:Mbs (Mus.Ms. 6448)

Falla, Manuel de (Spanish, 1876–1946)

Fanfare (1934)
wind and percussion
MS [G5]

Ferguson, Howard (English, b. 1908)

(2) *Fanfares* (1952)
4 trumpets, 3 trombones
MP (London: Boosey & Hawkes)

Finke, Fidelio (German, b. 1891)

Mein Trinklied
male voices and winds
MS [G5]

Festmusik for winds
MP (Breitkopf & Härtel)

Flament, Edouard (French, 1880–1958)

Fantaisie et Fugue, Op. 28,
1112-01, Eng. Horn
MP (Paris: Evette)

Ouverture dramatique, Op. 149
military band
MS [MGG]

6eme Symphonie, Op. 123
military band
MS [MGG]

Concerto Nr. 3, Op. 150
piano and military band
MS [MGG]

Fantasia con fuga, Op. 28
Wind instruments
MS [MGG]

Divertimento, Op. 137
6 bassoons
MS [MGG]

Divertimento Nr. 3, Op. 153, (on a theme by Czerny)
clarinet sextet
MS [MGG]

Frid, Géza (Hungarian, b. 1904)

Variations sur un theme néerlandais (1949)
band [later arranged for orchestra]
MS [G5]

Frischenschlager, Friedrich (Austrian, b. 1885)

Das feurige Männlein
male voices and percussion
MS [G5]

Frommel, Gerhard (German, b. 1906)

Suite, Op. 18 (1944)
8 winds
MP (Süddeutscher Musikverlag)

Concertino, Op. 24 (1943)
tenorhorn and 5 winds
MS [MGG]

Gál, Hans (Austrian, b. 1890)

Divertimento, Op. 22 (1924)
wind octet
MS [MGG, G5]

Galindo, Blas (Mexican, b. 1910)

Sextet (1941)
Wind instruments
Ms [G5]

Gebhard, Ludwig (German, b. 1907)

Suite, Op. 6
brass, percussion and piano
MS [MGG]

Gerhard, Roberto (Spanish, b. 1896)

Sardana I (1930)
'Katalon. Cobla-ensemble'
MS [G5]

Sardana II (1930)
eleven winds
MS [MGG]

German, Edward (German, 1862–1936)

Serenade
singer, winds and piano
MS [MGG]

Ghisi, Federico (Italian, b. 1901)

Sequenza e Giubile (1945)
chorus, winds, piano and percussion
MS [MGG]

Goller, Vinzenz (Austrian, 1873–1953)

Stephans-Messe, Op. 8
chorus, organ and winds
MS [MGG]

Loreto-Messe, Op. 25
chorus, organ and winds
MS [MGG]

Aloysius-Messe, Op. 34
chorus, organ and winds
MS [MGG]

Ordinarium Messae II, Op. 81
tenor, chorus, organ and winds
MS [MGG]

Oster Te deum, Op. 94
chorus, organ and 6 winds
MS [MGG]

Missa 'Anno Santo,' Op. 111
chorus, organ and 6 winds
MS [MGG]

(2) *Festfanfaren* (on a theme by Bruckner)
11 winds (on a theme by Bruckner)
MP (Vienna: Universal Edition)

Turmblasen
6 winds
MP (Vienna: Universal Edition)

Goosens, Eugene (English, b. 1893)

Fantasy, Op. 36 (1924)
1122-12
MS [G5]

Fanfare for a Regiment (1930)
4 trumpets, 4 trombones and percussion
MS [G5]

Grabner, Hermann (German, b. 1886)

Sonnengang
male voices and wind orchestra
MP (Düsseldorf: Schwann)

'Ein feste Berg,' cantata
chorus and trombone choir
MP (Leipzig: Kahnt)

Perked-Suite
wind orchestra
MP (Leipzig: Kahnt)

Burgmusik
wind orchestra
MP (Leipzig: Kahnt)

Firlefei-Variations
wind orchestra
MP (Leipzig: Kahnt)

Wilhelm Busch Suite
6 winds
MP (Leipzig: Kahnt)

Grainger, Percy (Australian, b. 1882)

Hill Song II (1907)
MS GB:Lbm (Add. 50870) full score

I'm Seventeen come Sunday (Setting Nr. 8)
MS GB:Lbm (Add. 50880)

Shepherd's Hey (Setting Nr. 20)
MS GB:Lbm (Add. 50881-2)

Duke of Marlborough (Lisbon, 1943)
MS GB:Lbm (Add. 50884)

Griffes, Charles (American, 1884–1920)

3 *Tone-Pictures*, Op. 5 (1910)
winds and harp [an arrangement by the composer]
MP (New York: Schirmer)

Grove, Stefans (German, b. 1922)

Turmmusik (1954)
brass
MS [MGG]

Grunewald, Jean-Jacques (French, b. 1911)

Messe héroïque (1945)
soli, chorus, 2 organs, 3 trumpets, 3 trombones and timpani
MS [MGG]

Haas, Joseph (German, 1879–1960)

Mass Nr. 1, Op. 80
unison chorus, winds and organ
MS [G5]

Mass Nr. 2, Op. 88
unison chorus, winds and organ
MS [G5]

Mass Nr. 4, Op. 96
unison chorus, winds and organ
MS [G5]

Speyeer Domfest Messe (1930, for the 900th anniversary of the Kaiserdom am Rhein)
unison chorus or audience, wind orchestra or organ
MS D:Mbs (Mus. Ms. 6562/Cim 448)

Halffter Escriche, Ernesto (Spanish, b. 1905)

Suite Ancienne for wind instruments
MS [G5]

Hansen, Jules

Overture triomphale, pour Harmonie
MP (Paris: Buffet, 1935)
    F:Pn (Ac.e.10.149)

Hanus, Jan (Czech, b. 1915)

Missa III (1955, Prag)
chorus, winds, timpani and organ
MS [MGG]

Harris, Roy (American, b. 1898)

Symphony for Band (1952)
MS (West Point Band Library) autograph score
    US:DW (copy at Trossingen)

Sammy's Fighting Sons
chorus and winds
MS [G5]

Red Cross Hymn
chorus and winds
MS [G5]

Cinnamon (1941)
band
MS [G5]

Folk Rhythms for Today (1941)
band
MS [G5]

Fruit of Gold (1949)
band
MS [G5]

Dark Devotion (1950
band
MS [G5]

Take the Sun and Keep the Stars (1944)
band
MS [G5]

Concerto (1941)
piano and band
MS [G5]

Fantasy (1941) f
piano and band
MS [G5]

Chorale (1944)
organ and brass
MS [G5]

Toccata (1944)
organ and brass
MS [G5]

Hasse, Karl (German, b. 1883)

Ouverture aus Kurland, Op. 20
wind orchestra
MS [MGG

Hartmann, R. E.

Riga-Tarnopol March (1915)
Band
MS D:Mbs (Mus.Ms. 11707)

Heiller, Anton (b. 1923)

Te deum (1954)
chorus, winds, timpani and organ
MP (Wien: Universal Edition)

Helenia, Hanns (German, b. 1890)

Lenz, Op. 18 (1907)
male choir and winds
MS [MGG]

Fanfare (1955)
6 winds and timpani
MS [MGG]

Henneberg, Carl Albert Wilhelm Richard (1853–1925)

Bläserserenade (Stockholm, 1918)
MS [MGG]

Henze, Hans Werner (German, b. 1926)

Concertino (1947)
piano, winds and percussion
MS [MGG, G5]

Herberigs, Robert (Belgian, b. 1886)

(2) *Suites* (1946)
3 trumpets, 4 horns and 3 trombones
MS [G5]

Herrmann, Hugo (German, b. 1896)

Festmusik (Ravensburg, 1929)
wind orchestra
MP (Leipzig: K & S)

Chw. Der Gemeinschaft, Op. 81
chorus, winds, piano and percussion
MP (Bote & Bock)

Morgenkant, Op. 40
chorus, winds and piano
MP (Heidelberg: Hochstein)

Deutsches Land, Op. 99
chorus, children's choir and wind orchestra
MP (published in Leipzig)

Sinfonia der Arbeit, Op. 90
wind orchestra
MP (Berlin: Bote & Bock)

Morgenhymne (1949)
winds
MS [MGG]

Hilber, Johann Baptist (Swiss, b. 1891)

Missa pro Patria (1941)
mixed chorus, brass and organ
MP (Cham: Willi)

Messe zu Ehren des HL Nilaaus v. Flüe (1947)
soli, mixed chorus, woodwinds, brass and organ
MP (Cham: Willi)

Proprium Missae SS. Trinitatis (1949)
chorus, winds or organ
MP (Edition Lucerna)

Musik zum Bundesfeierspiel (1941)
chorus and winds
MS [MGG]

Hlobil, Emil (Czech, b. 1901)

Okett , Op. 52 (1956)
winds
MS [MGG]

Hindemith, Paul (German, 1895–1963)

Konzertmusik, Op. 41
Wind orchestra
MS D:Mbs (Mus.Ms. Auto. P. Hindemith 1) Autograph score

Höffer, Paul (German, 1895–1949)

Festliche Ouverture (1937)
wind orchestra
MP (Berlin: Vieweg)

Flieggermusik (1937)
wind orchestra
MP (Leipzig: K & S)

Heitere Bläsersinfonie (1940)
MP (Leipzig: K & S)

Heitere Ouverure (1941)
wind orchestra
MP (Berlin: Vieweg)

Blasersextett, Op. 9
MS [MGG]

Holst, Gustav (English, 1874–1934)

The following autograph manuscripts are found in GB:Lbm.

Marching Song
band
MS (Add. 57871)

Music for a Pageant
band
MS (Add. 57876)

Hammersmith
band
MS (Add. 57904)

Bach's Fugue a la Gigue (1928)
band
MS (Add. 57909)

Suite in E♭
band
MS (Add. 47824)

Suite in F
band
MS (Add. 47825)

Moorside Suite
brass band
MS (Add. 47832)

Mr. Shilkret's Maggot
jazz orchestra
MS (Add. 47833)

Hoof, Jef Van (Belgian, b. 1886)

Missa, 'De Deo' (1937)
chorus and brass
MS [MGG]

Te Deum (1949)
chorus and brass
MS [MGG]

Rhythmische Suite (1923)
brass
MS [MGG]

Herr Halewyn (1930)
brass
MS [MGG]

Naar Ostland (1930)
brass
MS [MGG]

Howells, Herbert (English, b. 1892)

Pageantry Suite (1934)
brass band
MS [G5]

Huber-Anderach, Theodor (German, b. 1885)

Festlische Musik, Op. 7
Harmonie orchestra,
MS [MGG]

Hummel, Joseph Friedrich (Austrian)

Hymne von Richard Ritter von Strele-Bärwangen (1901)
SATB chorus and wind orchestra
MS A:Sca (Hs. 576)

Humpert, Hans (German, 1901–1943)

Hymne an die Arbeit, Cantata
chorus and wind orchestra
MS [MGG]

d'Indy, Vincent (French)

La vengeance du mari, (1931)
SATB and wind orchestra
MS F:Pn (MS. 9232)

Ippisch, Franz (German, b. 1883)

Symphonic Variations (1936)
wind orchestra
MS [MGG]

Ippolitow, Iwanow, Cichail Michailowirsch (Russian, 1859–1935)

Phythagoraische Hymne an die aufgehende Sohne, Op. 39
chorus, 10 flutes, 7 clarinets and 2 harps
MP (Moskau: Jurgenson)

Ireland, John (English, b. 1879)

A Downland Suite (1932)
brass band
MP (London: R. Smith, 1932)
MS GB:Lbm (Add. 52872) autograph score

A Maritime Overture (1944)
band
MP (London: Boosey & Hawkes, 1946)
MS GB: Lbm (Add. 52877) autograph condensed score

A Comedy Overture (1934)
brass band
MP (London: R. Smith, 1934)

Ives, Charles (American, 1874–1954)

December (1913)
unison chorus and winds
MS [MGG]

General William Booth's Entrance Into Heaven (1914)
chorus and winds
MS [MGG]

Jaeggi, Oswald (German, b. 1913)

Kleine Marien Kantate (1950)
chorus, winds, timpani and organ
MS [MGG]

James, Philip (American, b. 1890)

Perstare et Praestare, Festmarsch (1942)
band
MP (New York: Chappel, 1947)

Overture 'E.F.G.' (1944)
band
MP (New York: Leeds, 1947)

Fanfare and Ceremonial, Festmarsch (1955)
Band
MP (unknown publisher in New York, 1956)

Jenny, Albert (1912-1992, organist)

Suite (1933)
13 winds
MS [MGG]

Jeremias, Otakar (Czech, b. 1892)

Prísaha (*Der Schwur*, 1932)
chorus with recitation, orchestra and band
MS [MGG]

Jersild, Jorgen (Danish, b. 1913)

At spille I Skoven, Serenade for winds (1947)
MP (Kopenhagen: Hansen, 1951)

Jochum, Otto (German, b. 1898)

Karfreitagskantata, Op. 35a
chorus and brass
MS [MGG]

Ostergage, Op. 35b (1932)
chorus and brass
MS [MGG]

Liebesspiegel, Op. 38 (1932)
chorus and wind sextet
MS [MGG]

Jolivet, André (French, b. 1905)

Défilé u. Soir (1937)
wind orchestra
MS [MGG]

Suite delphine (1942)
1110-121, Martenot, harp, timpani and percussion
MP (Paris: Pathe-Marconi, 1957)

Jones, Daniel (Welsh, b. 1912)

Epicedium (1950)
chorus and 18 winds
MS [MGG, G5]

Septet (1949)
winds
MS [MGG, G5]

Nonett (1950)
winds
MS [MGG, G5]

Jongen, Joseph (Belgian, 1873–1953)

Piéce Symphonique (1930)
piano and wind orchestra
MS [G5]

Mass
solo voices, chorus, brass and organ
MS [G5]

Joubert, John (South African, b. 1927)

Divertimento (1951)
woodwinds, brass and percussion
MS [G5]

Kabelác, Miloslav (Czech, b. 1908)

Neustupuite ['Do not give way'] Cantata, Op. 7 (1939)
male chorus, brass and percussion
MS [G5]

Dechovy, Op. 8 (1940)
wind sextet
MS [G5]

Symphony, Op. 31 (1957)
wind orchestra, organ and timpani
MS [MGG]

Kallenberg, ? (1867–1944)

Komm spring mit mir (ca. 1920–1930)
soprano, tenor, 1111-04, Eng. hn
MS D:Mbs (Mus.Ms. 7787) Autograph score

Kallstenius, Edvin (Swedish, b. 1881)

Suite for 14 winds and timpani, Op. 23 (1938)
14 winds and timpani, revised in 1948 as a suite for orchestra, Op. 23c
MS [MGG]

Kaminski, Heinrich (German, 1886–1946)

Der Soldat
SATB, 3 trumpets, 3 horns, percussion
MS [MGG]

Karajew, Kara Abdulfas (Russian, b. 1918)

Sportsuite (1939)
wind orchestra
MS [MGG]

Kaufmann, Armin (Romanian, b. 1902)

Musik (1941) Op. 50
six solo winds and chamber orchestra
MS [MGG or G5?]

Kauffmann, Leo (German, 1901–1944)

Musik (1941)
3 trumpets, 4 horns, 3 trombones and tuba
MS D:Mbs (Mus.Ms App1115) Autograph score

Der 57 Psalm (1933)
alto, chorus, 6 winds and organ
MS D:Mbs (Mus.Ms. 8177) Autograph score

(6) *Blasermusiken*
3 trumpets, 4 horns, 3 trombones
MS D:Mbs (Mus.Ms. 8135)
    There are also additional unspecified wind compositions under Mus.Ms. 8136.

Kayser, Leif (Danish, b. 1919)

(8) *piccolo pezzi per banda* (1956)
MS [MGG]

Kelderfer, Viktor (b. 1873)

Festliche Musik
brass, organ and timpani
MP (Vienna: Österr. Bundesverlag, 1954)
    The score consists of an Intrada, Choral, Passacoglia & Fugue.

Hymnus (Vienna, 1924)
soli, chorus, winds, timpani, harp and organ
MS [MGG]

Klami, Uuno (Finish, b. 1900)

Finnish Cavalry March, Op. 28 (1939)
MS [G5]

Finnish Military March, Op. 42 (1950)
MS [G5]

Knab, Armin (German, 1881–1951)

Der deutsche Morgen
male chorus and wind orchestra
MP (Heidelberg: Hochstein, 1933)

Til Eulenspiegel (1950)
male chorus and winds
MP (Tonger, 1956)

Koechlin Charles (French, 1867–1950)

Choral pour une fête populaire (1935)
wind orchestra
MS (location unknown to widow)

Prelude a une fête populaire (1935)
wind orchestra
MS (location unknown to widow)

La victoire (1935)
wind orchestra
MP (Paris: Editions Sociales Internationales)
    US:DW (1314)

Jeux (1935) for wind orchestra
    (Paris: Editions Sociales Internationales)
    US:DW (1313)

Les Eaux vives (1936)
military band
MS [*Fête de la Lumiere*, 1937 Paris Exhibition]

Septet
IIII-0I, Eng. hn, saxophone
MS

(20) *Sonneries pour trompes de chasse*, Op. 123 (1932)
MP [MGG, G5]

(20) *Sonneries pour de chasse*, 2. serie, Op. 142 (1935)
MP [MGG, G5]

Chanson de Louis XIII
band
MS US:DW (181)

Koffler, Jozef (Polish, 1896–1943)

Symphony Nr. 3
wind instruments
MS [G5]

Komma, Karl Michael (Czech, b. 1913)

Psalmkantata (1958)
chorus, winds, harp
MS [MGG]

Konjus, Georgij Eduardowitsch (Russian, 1862–1933)

Serenade
7 winds
MS [MGG]

Kósa, György (Hungarian, b. 1897)

Hiob, biblische Kantata (1933)
baritone, 303-103
MS [MGG]

(6) *Portraits* (1933)
6 horns and harp
MS [MGG]

Kraft, Karl Joseph (b. 1903)

Missa C moll
SSATBB, brass and organ
MS D:Mbs (40Mus.Pr.44267)

Missa Psallite Deo, Op. 87 (1950)
chorus, 6 woodwinds or organ
MS [MGG]

Concerto breve, Nr. 2
brass and organ
MS [MGG]

Kraus, Hermann (German)

Bayern-Ruhm, Armee-Marsch (1918)
MS D:Mbs (Mus.Ms. 11709)

Kremenliev, Boris Angeloff (Bulgarian, b. 1911)

Three Village Sketches (1950)
wind orchestra
MS [MGG]

Piano Concerto (1950)
piano and wind orchestra
MS [MGG]

Wilderness Road (1953)
wind orchestra
MS [MGG]

Facing West from California's Shores (1954)
chorus and wind orchestra
MS [MGG]

Kronsteiner, Hermann (German, b. 1914)

Te deum (1946)
soli, chorus, winds and organ
MS [MGG]

Kundigraber, Hermann (German, 1879–1944)

Serenade, Op. 29
6 solo winds
MS [MGG]

Kuula, Toivo (Finnish, 1883–1918)

Lapua March, Op. 5
brass band
MS]G5]

(5) *Pieces*, Op. 28
brass band
MS [G5]

Karboraattorien marssi, Op. 33
brass band
MS [G5]

Lach, Robert (Austrian, 1874–1958)

Blaserseptett
MS A:Wn

(4) *Suites*
winds
MS A:Wn

Septett
winds and piano
MS A:Wn

Lahmer, Ruel (American, b. 1912)

The Campbells are coming (1948)
chorus and military band
MS [G5]

Lamote de Grignon, Ricardo (Spanish, b. 1899)

Joan de l'Os
soli, chorus and winds

Lampe, Walther (German, b. 1872)

Serenade, Op. 7 (1904)
15 winds
MP (Simrock)

Landowska, Wanda (Polish, b. 1879)

Polish Songs, composed for *das Orfeó Catalá, Barcelano*
soloists, chorus and wind orchestra
MS [MGG]

Fanfare de la Liberation
military orchestra
MS [MGG]

Langlais, Jean (French, b. 1907)

Mass Sale Regina (1954)
2 choirs, 2 organs and brass
MP A:Gk (uncataloged, in the attic)

Lastra, Erich Eder de (Austrian, fl. 1970s)

Second Symphony
wind orchestra
MS A:Gk (uncataloged, in the attic)

Lazzari, Sylvio (Austro-Italian, 1857–1944)

Octuer (1920)
1101-92, Eng. hn.
MP (Paris: Evette & Buffet)

Leleu, Jeanne (French, b. 1898)

Suite symphonique (Rome, 1925)
winds, piano and percussion
MS [MGG]

Levy, Ernst (German, b. 1895)

De Profundis (1919)
chorus, brass and organ
MS [MGG]
Hymnus Symphonicus (1936)
chorus brass and organ
MS [MGG]

Louel, Jean (Belgian, b. 1914)

Fanfare (1948)
brass
MS [G5]

Lutyens, Elisabeth (English, b. 1909)

Ballet (1949)
9 winds and percussion
MS [G5]

Madetoja, Leevi (Finnish, 1887–1947)

(3) *Pieces,* Op. 67, (1929)
band
MS [G5]

Ouverture-Fantasie, Op. 69, (1930)
band
MS [G5]

Malhebe, Edmond Henry (French, b. 1870)

Sextuor, Op. 31
winds
MS [G5]

Marchant, Stanley (English, 1883–1949)

Te Deum ('Solemn Thanksgiving,' 1931)
chorus, brass and organ
MS [G5]

Marteau, Henri (French)

Serenade, Op. 20
winds
MS [MGG]

Martin, Frank (Swiss, b. 1890)

La Nique à Satan (1932), *Spectacle populaire*
chorus, female chorus, children's chorus, wind orchestra,
   2 pianos
MS [MGG]

Martinu, Bohuslav (Czech, 1890–1959)

Feldmesse (1939)
baritone, male chorus, winds and percussion
MS [MGG]

Concerto
cello and wind orchestra
MS [MGG]

Marx, Karl (German, b. 1897)

Divertimento, Op. 21
16 winds
MS [MGG]

Mellers, Wilfrid (English, b. 1914)

Motets in Diem Pacis (1946)
chorus and brass
MS [MGG]

Migot, Georges (French, b. 1891, Superintendent of the Instrument Collection of the Paris Conservatory)

Symphonie pour 10 instruments à vent (1948)
MS [MGG]

Sinfonia da chiesa (1956), for wind orchestra
MS [MGG]

Mohaupt, Richard (German, 1904–1957)

Stadtpfeifermusik (1939), arranged (1953) for wind orchestras
MS [MGG]

McPhee, Colin (American, b. 1901)

Concerto (1928)
piano and 8 winds
MP (San Francisco: New Music)

Merikanto, Frans Oskar (Finnish, 1868–1924)

3 Stücke und 2 Festfanfaren
brass
MS [MGG]

Messner, Joseph (Austrian, b. 1893)

Messe in D, Op. 4 (Innsbruck, 1920)
chorus, winds and organ
MS [MGG]

Te deum, Op. 38 (Augsburg, 1935)
soprano, baritone, chorus and winds
MS [MGG]

Wechselgse. für das Fest Peter und Paul, Op. 7 (1925)
soli, chorus and winds
MS [MGG]

Festfanfaren, Op. 36b
6 winds and organ
MS (Augsburg: Böhm, 1933)

Salzburger Festspielfanfaren (1936)
winds
MS [MGG]

Mirouze, Marcel

Piéce en Septuor (1933)
IIII-II, piano
MS F:Pn (Ac.e.7.7)

Mohr, Jean-Baptiste-Victor

Air Varié
cornet and orchestra d'harmonie, or piano
MP (Paris: Lableur, 1867)
    F:Pn (K. 35664) piano part only

(8) *Morceaux pour musique d'Infantrie et cavalerie*
MP (Paris: Moncelot, 1855)
    F:Pn (D. 4336 [16])
    Contains 7 volumes of waltzes, polkas, and an *Air Varié* for solo E♭ clarinet and band.

Quatour
SATB saxophones
MP (Paris: A. Sax, 1864)
    F:Pn (K. 10.242)

Mohler, Philipp (German, b. 1908)

Leben, Präludium, Op. 5
male chorus, brass and timpani
MP (Heidelberg: Hochstein, 1936)

Monnikendam, Marius (Dutch?, b. 1896)

Veni Creator (1957)
male chorus and wind orchestra
MS [MGG]

Six Noëls (1957)
male chorus, children's chorus and wind orchestra
MS [MGG]

Ballade des Pendus (1949)
male chorus, brass and percussion
MS [MGG]

Missa Solemnissima (1959
chorus 7 brass and organ
MS [MGG]

Morera, Enrique (Spanish, 1865–1942)

Patria, march for wind orchestra
MS [MGG]

Moser, Franz (Austrian, 1880–1942)

Fest-Fanfare for large brass choir
MS A:Wn (Sm 21235)

Fest-Fanfare for large brass choir
MS A:Wn (Sm 21236)

Fest-Fanfare, for large brass choir
MS A: Wn (Sm 21237)

Marsch, Op. 10
wind orchestra
MS A:Wn

(6) *Märsche für Österreich Armeé*, Op. 16
MS A:Wn

(6) *Märsche für Preusische Armeé*
MS A:Wn (Sm 21171)

Scherzo, Op. 46
12 trumpets and bass trumpet
MS A:Wn

Moser, Rudolf (German, b. 1892)

Ode an die Allmacht, Op. 96 (1957)
chorus, brass and timpani
MS [MGG]

Suite, op. 84
Harmoniemusik
MS [MGG]

Moyzes, Mikulás (Slovakian, 1872–1944)

Wind sextet (1935)
MS [MGG]

Müller, Walter (Czech, b. 1899)

The 10th Psalm, Op. 43 (1939)
male chorus and winds
MS [MGG]

Neumann, Frantisek (Czech, 1874–1929)

Wind Octet
MS [MGG]

Nigg, Serge (French, b. 1924)

Concertino pour piano, winds and percussion (1947)
MP (Paris: Le Chant du Monde)

Nuffel, Julius (German, 1883–1953)

Dominus regnavit
chorus and wind orchestra
MS [MGG]

Otterloo, Willem van (Dutch, b. 1907)

Sinfonietta (1943) for 16 winds
MP [MGG]

Intrada (1958
brass [MGG]

Divertimento (1946)
brass, piano, celesta and percussion
MS [MGG]

Palester, Roman (Polish, b. 1907)

Children's Symphony (1933)
6 winds and percussion
MS [G5]

Pnaufnik, Tomasz (Polish, 1876–1951)

5 Polish songs (1940)
children's chorus and wind ensemble
MP (London: Bo & Ma, 1957, according to MGG)

Papandopulo, Boris (Croatian, b. 1906)

Concerto da Camera, Op. 11 (1929)
soprano, 1221-, piccolo, Eng. hn, bass clarinet, violin and piano
MP (Vienna: Universal Edition)

Pentland, Barbara (b. 1912)

Octet for winds (1948)
MS [MGG]

Pepping, Ernst (German, b. 1901)

Kleine Serenade
military band (1926, Donaueschingen)
MS [MGG]
       This score is in the West Point Band Library.

Concerto I (1926)
viola, 202-202, 4 string bass
MS [MGG]

Concerto II (1926)
clarinet, trombone and 6 winds
MS [MGG]

Pérez, Casas (Spanish, 1873–1956)

Stücke für Militär-Orchestra
MS [MGG]

Petridis, Petro (Greek, b. 1892)

Concerto grosso (1929)
winds and timpani
MS [G5]

Petyrek, Felix (Austrian, b. 1892)

Divertimento
8 winds
MS [G5]

Pijper, Willem (Dutch, 1894–1947)

Op den Weefstoel (1918)
chorus 2222-01, piano 4-hand
MS [MGG]

Réveillez-vous, Piccars (1932)
male chorus and winds
MS [MGG]

Pilati, Mario (Italian, 1903–1938)

Divertimento (1932)
3 trumpets, 4 horns, 2 trombones
MS [MGG]

Pizzetti, Ildebrando (Italian, b. 1880)

Cantico di Gloria (1848)
3 choirs, 24 winds, 2 pianos, percussion
MS [MGG, G5]

Porter, Quincy (American, b. 1897)

Concertino (1959), for wind orchestra
MS [MGG]

Racek, Fritz (Czech, b. 1911)

Symphonic Suite (Vienna, 1952)
winds, percussion and organ
MS [MGG[]]

Rakow, Nikolai (Russian, b. 1908)

Various unnamed works for wind orchestra, according to MGG.

Rasse, François (1873–1955)

Three works for wind orchestra according to MGG.

Rathaus, Karol (Hungarian, 1895–1954)

Divertimento, Op. 73
10 winds
MS [MGG]

Reger, Max (German, 1873–1916)

Serenade (1908)
2222-04
MS A:Wgm (VIII 56.413) Autograph score

Hochgieblig Haus (1906)
SATB, 2222-04, timpani
MS [MGG]

Reiner, Karel (Czech, b. 1910)

Suite concertante (1948)
winds and percussion
MS [MGG]

Reizenstein, Franz (English, b. 1911)

Serenade (1951)
1202-02, string bass
MS (Boosey & Hawkes)

Reub, August (German, 1871–1935)

Oktett, Op. 37 (1918)
222-02
MS [MGG]

Reutter, Hermann (German, b. 1900)

Six Choruses from Calderon's Grobes Welttheater (1951)
wind orchestra
MS [MGG]

Riegger, Wallingford (American, b. 1885)

Music for Brass Choir (1948)
MS [G5]

Riisager, Knudage (Danish, b. 1897)

Sinfonietta (1924
8 winds
MS [MGG]

Ringbom, Nils-Eric (Finnish, b. 1907)

Sextett (1951) for winds
MS [MGG]

Rocca, Lodovico (Italian, b. 1895)

Salmodia
baritone, small chorus, 11 winds and percussion
MP (Milan: Riccordi, 1934)

Rogalski, Theodor (Romanian, 1901–1954)

2 Tänze (1925)
winds, percussion and piano 4-hand
MP (Bukarest: Verlag der Ges. Rumän. Komp)

Rogister, Jean (Belgian, b. 1879)

Oktett for winds
MS [MGG]

Roussel, Albert (French, 1869–1937)

Fanfare pour un sacre païen (1921)
brass and timpani
MS F:Pn (MS.10.160)
MP (Paris: Durand, 1941)
    F:Pn (MS.10.160)

A Glorious Day, Op. 48 (1932)
military band
MS F:Pn (MS.10.160)
MP (Paris: Durand, 1933)
    F:Pn (MS.10.165)

Le Bardit des Francs (1926)
unaccompanied male chorus or winds and percussion
MS [MGG]

Salzedo, Carlos (b. 1885, French harpist)

Concerto (1926)
harp and 7 winds
MS [G5]

Sanders, Robert (American, b. 1906)

Symphony for Band (1943)
MS [G5]

Scelsi, Giacinto (Italian, b. 1905)

Rotative (1931)
3 pianos, winds and percussion
MS [G5]

Schelb, Josef (German, b. 1894)

Das Kroninger Brunnenlied
folk chorus and wind orchestra
MS [MGG]

Solo Concerto
flute, oboe, clarinet, bass clarinet, trumpet, horn, trombone, 6 solo winds and percussion
MS [MGG]

Festlicher Marsch
large wind orchestra
MP (Heidelberg: Müller)

Schillings, Max (German, 1868–1933)

Festlicher Marsch, Op. 27 (1911)
military band
MS [G5]

Schiske, Karl (Austrian, b. 1916)

Trompetermusik (1940)
brass and percussion
MS [G5]

Schmid, Erich (Swiss, b. 1907)

Suite, Op. 7 (1931)
wind band and percussion
MS [G5]

Schmidt, Franz (Austrian, 1874–1939)

Zutritt
6 trumpets, 3 horns, 3 trombones, tuba, timpani
MP (Vienna: Doblinger, 1959)

Lied. Ländler, Marsch (1904–1907)
2 oboes, 2 trumpets, 4 horns, tuba or bassoon and percussion
MS [MGG]

Variations and Fuge (first version, Vienna, 1925)
wind ensemble; second version, Vienna, 1927, for 14 winds, organ and timpani
MS [MGG]

'Gott erhalte' (1933)
ad. lib. Wind choir
MS [MGG]

Schmitt, Florent (French, 1870–1958)

Hymne funébre, Op. 46
SATB, tenor solo, orchestra l'harmonie.
MS F:Pn (Cons.MS.14516)

This is a 24 page autograph score for a very large wind orchestra, with pencil and red ink corrections.

Marche de la classes en Route Vers libres Azurs (August, 1894)
MS   F:Pn (Cons. MS.13575) autograph score
    This is a good composition for large band, but it carries a note on the catalog card reading, 'this has not been published, according to the desire of the composer.'

Marche du CLXIII pour musique militaire, Op. 48, Nr. 2 (Feb., 1916)
MS   (Paris: Durand, 1918)
    F:Pn (Aa.47618)

Schoeck, Othmar (Swiss, b. 1886)

Cantata, Op. 49 (1933)
baritone, male chorus, brass, piano and percussion
MS [G5]

Schreck, Gustav Ernst (German, 1849–1918)

Nonett, Op. 40
2122-02
MP (Leipzig: Breitkopf & Härtel)

Schultz, Svend (Danish, b. 1913)

Job, Oratorio
chorus, wind orchestra and harp
MP (Kopenhagen: Samfundet til Udigivelse af dansk Musik, 1947)

Schumann, Erich (b. 1989)

Marches for Symphonic Wind Orchestra
MS [MGG]

Schwarz-Schilling, Reinhard (German, b. 1904)

Intrade (1958)
10 brass
MS [MGG]

Signum magnum (1958)
chorus, 4 trumpets, 4 horns, 4 trombones
MS [MGG]

Scontrino, Antonia (Italian, 1850–1922)

Adagio
voice and wind
MS [may be at the Conservatory at Palermo]

Sehlbach, Erich (German, b. 1898)

Turnmusiken, for brass
MS [MGG]

Sekles, Bernhard (German, 1872–1934)

Variations on 'Prinz Eugen,' Op. 32
male choir, winds and percussion
MS [G5]

Siklós, Albert (Hungarian, 1878–1942)

Septett (1938)
winds
MS [MGG]

Sextett
winds and harp
MS [MGG]

Skalkotas, Nicos (Greek, 1904–1949)

Classical Symphony (1947)
Wind Orchestra
MP (Teilauff, 1947)

Concerto (1939)
Wind Instruments
MS [MGG]

Octet (before 1943, now lost)
winds
MS [MGG]

Spisak, Michal (Polish, b. 1914)

Aubade (1949)
wind orchestra
MS [MGG]

Staempfli, Edward (Swiss, b. 1908)

Liberté (1944)
soli, chorus, brass, timpani and piano
MS [MGG]

Variations (1950)
13 winds
MS [MGG]

Five Pieces for Woodwinds (1946)
MS [MGG]

Four Pieces for Brass Instruments (1946)
MS [MGG]

Stanford, Charles Villiers (English, 1852–1924)

March Op. 108 (1892)
wind instruments
MS [MGG]

Stevens, Bernard (English, b. 1916)

'East' and 'West' Overture, Op. 16 (1950)
wind band
MS [G5]

Studer, Hans (Swiss, b. 1911)

Concerto (1952)
organ, winds and percussion
MS [MGG]

Divertimento
winds and double bass
MS [G5]

Sturzenegger, Richard (Swiss, b. 1905)

Festspiel (1949)
chorus, wind orchestra and organ
MS [MGG]

Stutschewsky, Joachim (German, b. 1891)

Sextett (1960)
1111-02
MS [MGG]

Suter, Robert (Swiss, b. 1919)

Balade v. den Seeräubern (Brecht, 1953)
male chorus, brass and percussion
MS [MGG]

Sutermeister, Heinrich (Swiss, b. 1910)

Son et Flamme (Lausanne, 1964)
chorus and wind orchestra
MS [MGG]

Szabelski, Bolslaw (Polish, b. 1896)

Marsz zolnierski (Soldatenmarsch, W. Broniewski, 1943)
chorus and wind orchestra
MS [MGG]

Tebaldini, Giovanni (Italian, 1864–1952)

Vexilla
TB, 2 cornets, 4 trumpets, 4 horns, 4 trombones, 2 flicorno and tuba
MS [MGG]

Thilman, Johannes Paul (German, b. 1906)

Das 7-Bläser-Stück
2 trumpets, 2 horns, 2 trombones and tuba
MS [MGG]

Thomson, Virgil (American, b. 1896)

A Solemn Music (1940, for band
MP [G5]

At the Beach (1949), concert waltz
trumpet and band
MS [G5]

Tittel, Ernst (German, b. 1910)

Missa, 'Magnus et potens' Op. 15
chorus, winds and organ
MP (Düsseldorf: Schwann, 1939)

Tovey, Donald (English, 1875–1940)

National March for the Sultan of Zanzibar
band
MS [G5]

Tschemberdshi, Nikolai Karpowitsch (1903–1948)

Marches
wind orchestra
MS [MGG]

Concertino for woodwinds (1935)
MS [MGG]

Uhl, Alfred (Austrian)

Concertino
violin and small wind orchestra
MS [MGG]

Vergnügliches Musik, for 222-02
     [MGG]

Verèse, Edgar (Franco-American, b. 1885)

Equatorial (1937)
bass-baritone voice, trumpets, trombones and organ, percussion, Theremin instrument
MS [G5]

Hyperprism
winds and percussion
MS [G5]

Vaughan Williams, Ralph (England, 1872-1958)

The following are autograph scores in GB:Lbm.
England my England
singer and band
(Add. 50464) [if ordering a microfilm request everything in this folder]

Overture, Henry V
brass band
(Add. 57288)

The Golden Vanity
band [unfinished]
(Add. 57288)

Flourish
band
(Add. 57489)

Toccata Marziale
band
(Add. 59796)

Variations
brass band
(Add. 50404-5) score and sketches

Vidal, Paul-Antoine (French, 1863–1931)

*Methode rapide à l'usage des instruments à vent pour les musiques d'harmonie et de fanfare, les écoles de
  musique* ... (1911)
MP (Paris: Leduc, 1912)

Vierne, Louis (French, 1870–1937)

Marche triomphale pour le centenaire de Napoleon
brass and timpani
MP (Paris: Salabert, 1921)

Villa-Lobos, Heiter (Brazil, 1887–1959)

According to MGG a chronological verzeichnis of the works of Villa-Lobos is available
  from the Panamerican Union, in Washington, D.C.

Paraguai (1904)
band
MS [G5]

Brasil (1905)
band
MS [G5]

Pre-Paz March (1912)
band
MS [G5]

Valsa brasileira (1918)
band
MS [G5]

Fantasia Brasilieria (1926)
band
MS [G5]

O Pião (1936)
band
     [G5]

Chôros, Nr. 3 (1925)
male chorus, clarinet, saxophone, bassoon, 3 horns and trombone
MS [G5]

Wagenaar, Johan (Dutch, 1862–1941)

Hymne
winds and organ
MS [MGG]

Wagner, Siegfried Richard (German, 1869–1930)

Wer liebt uns (1924, Bayreuth)
male chorus and winds
MS [MGG]

Walter, Karl (Austrian, 1862–1929)

Weihnachtsmesse
chorus, folk-chorus, winds and organ
MP (Düsseldorf: Schwann, 1941)

Festmesse (1958)
chorus, winds and organ
MP (Vienna: Doblinger)

Deutsches Proprium zum Fest des hl. Bernardus (1964)
chorus, winds and organ
MS [MGG]

Deutsches Proprium für das Kreuzerhöhungfest (1952)
chorus, winds and organ
    [MGG]

Weber, Ludwig (German, 1891–1947)

Musik
brass and organ
MP (Augsburg: Filser, 1928)

Wehrli, Werner (Swiss, 1892–1944)

Antike Strophen (1944)
unison male chorus and winds
MS [G5]

Weichowicz, Stanislaw (Polish, b. 1893)

Dzien slowianski (A Slovanic Day, 1929), cantata
chorus and wind orchestra
MS [G5]

Weill, Kurt (German, 1900–1950)

Concerto, Op. 12 (1925)
violin and wind orchestra
MS [MGG]

Vom Tod im Wald, Op. 16 (1927)
bass and 10 winds
MS [MGG]

Das Berliner Requiem (Brecht, 1928)
male choir and winds
MS [MGG]

Weinzweig, John (Canadian, b. 1913)

Divertimento (1961)
trumpet, trombone and wind orchestra
MS [MGG]

Wildgans, Friedrich (German, 1913–1965)

Konzert, Op. 31b
organ, brass and percussion
MS [MGG]

Winter, Paul (German, 1894–1971)

2 *Fanfares* (for the Winter Olympics, 1935)
MS D:Mbs (Mus.Ms 6554) Autograph score
MP (Regensbrg:Bosse)
    copy in D:Mbs (Mus.Pr.40-19731)

Fanfare for the Berlin Olympics, 1936
4 trumpets, 2 alto horns, 3 trombones, tuba and timpani
MS D:Mbs (Mus.Ms. 5363) Autograph

Wohlfahrt, Frank (German, b. 1894)

Sancta Trinitas
chorus, piano, cello, string bass, wind orchestra
MS [MGG]

Wood, Ralph (English, b. 1901)

Dissegno (1959)
wind orchestra
MS [MGG]

Wood, Thomas (English, 1892–1950)

Cantata (for the Festival of Britain, 1951)
baritone, chorus, brass ensemble
MS [MGG]

Wöss, Josef Venantius von (Austrian, 1863–1943)

Missa in adorat. SS Trinitatis, Op. 45
chorus, wind orchestra and timpani
MP (Vienna: Universal Edition)

Zbinden, Julien-François (Swiss, b. 1917)

Concerto de Gibraltar
piano and brass
MS [MGG]

Zender, Hans (German, b. 1936)

Vexilla Regia (1964)
soprano, flute, trumpet, winds, timpani and organ
MS [MGG]

Ziegler, Benno (German, 1891–1965)

Um Mitternacht
TTBB, brass
MS D:Mbs (Mus.Ms. 8901) Autograph score, 1923

Zillig, Winfried (German, 1905–1963)

Serenade Nr. 1 (1927)
8 brass
MS [MGG]

Zoras, Leonidas (Greek, b. 1905)

Konzertino (1950)
violin and 11 woodwinds
[MGG]

Early Twentieth-Century Repertoire
for Five or Fewer Wind Players

Abranyi, Emil (Hungarian, b. 1882)

Andante e Minuetto (1900)
wind instruments
MS [G5]

d'Albert, Eugen (Scottish-German, 1864–1932)

Flauto solo (Prag, 1905)
MS [MGG]

Atterburg, Kurt Magnus (Swedish, b. 1887)

Concerto for horn and orchestra
MP (Breitkopf & Härtel)

Baussnern, Waldemar (German, 1866–1931)

Wer weiss wo
baritone solo, male chorus, 2 trumpets, 2 horns, trombones and timpani
MP (Essen: Rheinischer Musikverlag)

Serenade
piano, violin, clarinet, horn and cello
MP (Berlin: Simrock, 1898)

Suite for piano and clarinet
MP (Berlin: Wieweg, 1925)

Bax, Arnold (English, 1883–1953)

Now is the time of Christymus (1921)
male chorus, flute and piano
MS [G5]

Beck, Conrad (Swiss, b. 1901)

Concert Music (1932
oboe ad string orchestra
MP (Schött)

Sonatine (1935) for flute and violin
MP (Salabet)

Serenade (1935)
flute, clarinet and string orchestra
MP (Schött)

Sonatine (1941)
oboe and piano
MS [G5]

Concerto (1941)
flute and orchestra
MS [G5]

Intermezzo (1948)
horn and piano
MP (Heugel)

Bedford, Herbert (English, 1867–1945)

Nocturne
6 female voices, horn, harp and percussion
MS [G5]

Bentzon, Jorgen (Danish, b. 1897)

Bläsertrio, Op. 7 (1924)
MP (Frankfurt: ISCM, 1927)

Sonate (1926) for bassoon, viola and violin
MS [MGG]

Intermezzo, Op. 24 (1933)
clarinet and violin
MS [MGG]

Sonatine (1945)
flute and piano
MS [MGG]

Rapsodie, Op. 10 (1925)
English horn
MS [MGG]

Variationen, Op. 14 (1927)
clarinet
MS [MGG]

Variationen, Op. 34 (1938)
bassoon
MS [MGG]

Bentzon, Niels (Danish, b. 1919)

Quintet, OP. 12 (1941)
winds and piano
MS [MGG]

2 *Wind Quartets*, OP. 29 (1943) and Op. 59 (1949)
MS [MGG]

Mosaique musical, Op. 54 (1948)
flute, violin and piano
MS [MGG]

Sonata, Op. 47 (1947)
horn
MS [MGG]

Sonata, OP. 63 (1950)
clarinet
MS [MGG]

Variationen, Op. 17 (1942)
flute and piano
MS [MGG]

2 *Stücke*, Op. 41 (1945)
oboe and piano
MS [MGG]

Berezovsky, Nicolay (b. 1900 in Russia)

2 *Woodwind Quintets*, Nr. 1, (1928) and Nr. 2 (1937)
MS [MGG]

Bialas, Gunter (b. 1907 in Prussian Silesia)

Concerto
flute and orchestra
MP (Heidelberg: Müller)

Sonate
flute and piano
MP (Heidelberg: Müller)

Gesang von den Tieren, Kammerkanate
alto, flute, clarinet, cembalo and percussion
MS [MGG]

Drei Chinese Gesange
flute and alto
MS [MGG]

Binet, Jean (Swiss, b. 1893)

Sonatine (1942)
alto and flute
MS [MGG]

Kaval (1945)
flute and piano
MS [MGG]

Borck, Edmund von (German, b. 1906)

Introduktion und Capriccio, Op. 11 (1935)
violin or alto saxophone and piano
MS [MGG]

Concertino, Op. 15b (1936)
flute and strings
MS [MGG]

Sextett, Op. 15a
flute and strings
MS [MGG]

Bowles, Paul (American, b. 1910)

Scènes d'Anabase (1932)
tenor, oboe and piano
MS [G5]

Bridge, Frank (English, 1879–1941)

4 Divertimenti (1934–1938)
flute, oboe, clarinet and bassoon
MS [MGG]

Bruneau, Louis Charles (France, 1957–1934)

Fantaisie (1901)
horn and piano
MS [MGG]

Brunetti-Pasano, August (Austrian, b. 1870)

Woodwind Quintet
MS A:Sca (Hs. 1176)

Quartet
4 flutes
MS A:Sca (Hs. 1177)

Elegie for flute and piano
MS A:Sca (Hs. 1190)

Brustad, Fjarne (b. 1895)

Trio Nr. 1 (1939)
clarinet, violin and viola
MS [MGG]

Trio Nr. 2 (1947)
violin, clarinet and bassoon
MS [MGG]

Burkhard, Willy (Swiss, b. 1900)

Choral duets, Op. 22 (1928)
male voices, trumpet and trombones
MS [G5]

Busser, Henri (French, b. 1872)

MGG lists some 25 compositions for single winds.

Canteloube, Joseph (French, b. 1879)

Rustiques Trio (1946)
oboe, clarinet and bassoon
MS [MGG]

Casadesus, Francis (French, b. 1870)

Romance provençale et danse
baritone saxophone and piano
MP (Paris: Lemoine)

Chapdevielle, Pierre (French, b. 1906)

Exercisme, Monodie (1936)
alto saxophone
MS [MGG]

Caplet, André (French, 1878–1925)

Quintett (1898)
1112-
MS [MGG]

Deux pieces (1897)
flute and piano
MP (Hustel)

Feuillets d'Album (1901)
flute and piano
MS [MGG]

Improvisations (1926)
flute and piano
MP (Durand)

Improvisations (1926)
clarinet and piano
MP (Durand)

Marche de la Division de Neuville (1916)
clarions, trumpet, percussion
MP (Durand)

Ecoute, mon Coeur
singer and flute
MS [MGG]

Carpentier, Raymond (b. 1880)

Quintett for winds
MS [MGG]

Casella, Alfredo (Italian, 1893–1947)

Siciliana e burlesca, Op. 23 (1914)
flute and piano
MS [MGG]

Chailley, Jacques (French, 1910–1936)

Barcarolle
wind quintet
MS [MGG]

Trois pieces en courte-pointe
flute and piano
MP (Paris: Leduc)

Chavez, Carlos (Mexican, b. 1899)

Soli (1933)
oboe, clarinet, bassoon and trumpet
MS [G5]

Tierra Mojada (1932)
chorus, oboe and English hn.
MS [G5]

Chemin-Petit, Hans (German, b. 1902)

Trio in alten Stil (1943)
oboe, clarinet and bassoon
MS [MGG]

Blaserquintett (1947)
MS [MGG]

Coleridge-Taylor, Samuel (English, 1875–1912)

Quintett, Op. 10,
clarinet and strings
MP (Breitkopf & Härtel)

Collier, Alexandre-Eugene (French, b. 1883)

Chevauchee Fantastique
trumpet and piano
MP (Paris: Costallet)

Ballade
horn and piano
MP (Paris: Leduc)

Choral varié sur le choral 'Christ est ressauscite' de Leo Hassler
4 trombones and organ [an arrangement]
MS [MGG]

Cinq danses ancienne [arr.]
IIII-OI
MS [MGG]

Cools, Eugene (French, 1877–1936)

Poéme for flute and orchestra
    [MGG]

Trois Pieces
flute and orchestra
MS [MGG]

Elegie
clarinet and orchestra
MS [MGG]

Sicilienne
flute and piano
MS [MGG]

Sonata
flute and piano
MS [MGG]

Cras, Jean (French, 1879–1932)

Quatuor (1924)
saxophones
MS [MGG]

Suite en duo (1927)
flute and harp
MP (Salabert)

Quintett (1928)
flute, harp and strings
MP (Salabert)

La Fluta de Pan (1928)
singer, flute and 3 strings
MP (Salabert)

David, Carl Heinrich (Swiss, 1884–1951)

Erstes Quartet (1934–1941)
alto saxophone, violin, cello and piano
MS [MGG]

Koncert
saxophone & string orchestra
MS [MGG]

Concertino
bassoon and strings
MP (Hug)

Duo (1951)
horn and piano
MS [MGG]

David, Johann Nepomuk (Austrian, b. 1895)

Cantata, Fröhlich wir non all'fangen an (1941)
soprano, contralto, bass, oboe and organ
MS [MGG]

Sonate, Op. 26 (1939)
flute, viola and lute
MS [MGG]

Trio, Op. 30 (1940),
flute, violin and viola
MS [MGG]

Solo-Sonaten (Op. 31), Nr. 1, for flute
MS [MGG]

Sonaten, Op. 32
    Nr. 1 for flute and viola (1943)
    Nr. 2 for Block-flute and lute (1943)
    Nr. 3 for clarinet and viola (1948)
MSS [MGG]

Degen, Helmut (German, b. 1911)

Koncert
organ and trombone choir
MS [MGG]

Trio (1950)
flute, viola and piano
MS [MGG]

Delannoy, Marcel-François-Georges (French, b. 1898)

Rapsodie
alto saxophone, trumpet, cello and piano
MP (Paris: Heugel, 1934)

Deux Poèmes d'A. Germain
singer, flute, piano and strong quartet
MS [MGG]

Dello Joio, Norman (American, b. 1913)

Mystic Trumpeter (1943)
chorus and horn
MS [G5]

Delmas, Marc (French, 1885–1931)

MGG attributes to Delmas various unnamed solo works for winds.

Donostia, P. Jose Antonio de (Spanish, b. 1886)

Poema de la passion
mixed chorus, 2 soprani, Eng. hn
MS [MGG]

Desderi, Ettore (Italian, b. 1892)

Suite
oboe, clarinet, horn, bassoon and piano
MS [MGG]

Diemer, Louis Joseph (French, 1843–1919)

Scherzo
winds and piano
MS [MGG]

Diepenbrock, Alphons (French, 1862–1921)

Come raggio di sol (1917)
wind quintet
MS [MGG]

Wenn ich ihn nur habe
wind quintet and string bass
MS [MGG]

Döbereiner, Christian (German, b. 1874)

Sonata
4 flutes, 2 Gamben, string bass
MP (Schott)

Dopper, Cornelis (Dutch, 1870–1939)

Sextett
piano and 5 winds [lost]
MS [MGG]

Dresden, Sem (Dutch, b. 1881)

Chorus tragicus
mixed chorus, trumpet, horn and percussion
MS [MGG]

Konzert for flute
MS [MGG]

Symphonietta
clarinet and orchestra
MS [MGG]

Suite
winds and piano
MS [MGG]

Dressel, Erwin (German, b. 1909)

Konzert (1951)
oboe, clarinet, bassoon and orchestra
MS [MGG]

Sonaren
flute and piano
MS [MGG]

Sonaten
clarinet and piano
MS [MGG]

Quartet (Dresden, 1933)
clarinet, violin, cello and piano
      [MGG]

Dubois, François-Clément-Théodore (French, 1837–1924)

2 *Suites* for winds (1898)
MS [MGG]

Fantasietta, for flute, violin, trumpet, horn, cello, harp, timpani and strings
MP (Paris: Heugel, 1914)

Dixteur (1909)
wind quintet and strings
MS [MGG]

Nonetto (1926
flute, clarinet, bassoon and strings
MS [MGG]

Ducasse, Roge-Jean-Jules Aimable (French, b. 1873)

Trio for oboe, clarinet and bassoon
MS [MGG]

Egge, Klaus (German, b. 1906)

Wind Quintet, Op. 13 (1939)
MS [MGG]

Ehrenberg, Karl Emil Theodor (German, b. 1878)

Quartet (1943)
oboe, clarinet, horn and bassoon
MS [MGG]

Eisenmann, Will (German-Swiss, b. 1906)

Nevermore
saxophone and piano (1940)
MP (Fisher)

Divertimento (1940)
flute, clarinet and bassoon
MS [MGG]

Duo Concertante (1941)
saxophone and piano
MS [MGG]

Ballade (1952)
flute and piano
MS [MGG]

Eisler, Hanns (German, b. 1898)

Wind quintet, Op. 4
MS [MGG]

Palmström, Op. 5 [*Studien ibe Zwölftonreihen in Form von Variationen*]
Sprechsinger, flute, clarinet, violin and cello
MS [MGG]

Elgar, Edward (English, 1857–1934)

Wind Quintets
2 flutes, oboe, clarinet and bassoon
MS GB:Lbm (Add. 58051; Add. 58052 [copies]; Add. 60316 A-E)

Elling, Catharinus (Norway, 1858–1942)

Konzertstykke (Oslo, 1916)
flute and orchestra
MS [MGG]

Emberg, Jens Laursh (b. 1879)

Tre smaa stykker, Op. 55
oboe, viola and cello
MS [MGG]

Drei Lieden mit Ritornellen, Op. 45
singer, clarinet and string quartet
MS [MGG]

Emmanuel, Maurice Marie François (French, 1862–1938)

Sonate, Op. 29 (1936)
cornet or signalhorn and piano
MP (Paris: Buffet Crampon)

Sonate, Op. 11 (1907)
clarinet, flute and piano
MP (Paris: Lemoine)

Trois edelettes anacréontiques, Op. 13 (1911)
singer, flue and piano
MP (Paris: Lemoine)

Erb, Marie-Joseph (French, 1858–1944)

MGG attributes to Erb unnamed works for saxophone quartet and for horn.

Erlanger, Camille (French, 1863–1919)

[unnamed composition]
trumpette chromatique in F and piano
MP (Paris: Evette et Schaeffer)

Ettinger, Markus Wolf (German, 1874–1951)

Konzert (1936)
horn, strings and timpani
MS [MGG]

Eysler, Edmond (German, 1874–1949)

Vier Stücke für Jazzmusik
MS [MGG]

Ferguson, Howard (English, b. 1908)

Four Short Pieces, Op. 6 (1937)
clarinet and piano
MS [MGG]

Three Sketches, Op. 14 (1953)
flute and piano
MS [MGG]

Five Pipe Pieces
Blockflute or Bambuspfeifen (1935)
MP (London: Cramer)

Fernandez, Oscar Lorenze (Brazilian, 1897–1948)

Quintett
IIII-OI
MS [MGG]

Ferroud, Piere Octave (French, 1900–1936)

Trio (1933)
oboe, clarinet and bassoon
MS [MGG]

Trio pieces pour flute seule (1921)
MS [MGG]

Flament, Edouard (French, 1880–1958)

Exercises techniques pour le bassoon, Op. 40
MS [MGG]

Quinze etudes pour le bassoon, Op. 140
MS [MGG]

Poème nocturne, Op. 7
piano and winds

Fantaisie, Op. 54
bassoon, violin and cello
MS [MGG]

1er Sextuer, Op. 109
flute, clarinet and strings
MS [MGG]

Suite, Op. 124
clarinet quartet
MS [MGG]

Suite, Op. 126
woodwind quintet
MS [MGG]

Trois pieces
woodwind trio
MS [MGG]

Concerto, Op. 132
bassoon and cello
MS [MGG]

Morceau de Concert, Op. 138
tuba and piano
MS [MGG]

2eme Quintete, Op. 139
5 bassoons
MS [MGG]

1er Quarteur, Op. 144
4 bassoons
MS [MGG]

Divertimento Nr. 2, Op. 146
oboe, oboe d'amore, Eng. hn and bassoon
MS [MGG]

Serenade Nr. 1
oboe, viola and harp
MS [MGG]

Serenade Nr. 2
flute, violin, cello and harp
MS [MGG]

Serenade Nr. 3, Op. 129
soprano, violin, viola, cello, flute and harp
MS [MGG]

Concertstücke, Op. 13
bassoon and orchestra
MS [MGG]

2eme Elegie, Op. 105
English horn and string orchestra
MS [MGG]

Foerster, Joseph Bohuslav (Czech, 1859–1951)

Blaserquintett, Op. 95
MS [MGG]

Frey, Emil (Swiss, 1889–1946)

Stücke for winds and piano, Op. 80, 81, 87, 88, 89
MS [MGG]

Froidebise, Piere-Jean-Marie (French, b. 1914)

Amercouer
singer, wind quintet and piano
MS [MGG]

Fromm-Michael, Ilse (German, b. 1888)

4 Puppen, Op. 4
piano; later arr. for wind quintet
MS [MGG]

Gaillard, Marius-François (French, b. 1900)

Noite sobre o Tejo (1934)
saxophone and piano
MP (Paris: Costallat)

Sylvestre (1950)
flute and piano
MP (New York: Baron)

Gallois-Montburn, Raymond (French, b. 1918)

Six pieces musicales d'etudes
saxophone and piano
MS [MGG]

Intermezzo for saxophone and piano
MS [MGG]

Gardner, John Linton (English, b. 1917)

Theme and Variations, Op. 7, (1951)
2 trumpets, horn and trombone
MP (London: OUP, 1953)

Five German Folksong Settings (1939)
flute, oboe and piano
MS [MGG]

Rhapsody (1935)
oboe and string quartet
MS [MGG]

Gensmer, Harald (German, b. 1909)

Cantata (1952)
tenor, flute and guitar
MS [MGG]

Geiser, Walther (German, b. 1897)

Danza notturna, Op. 36a (1947)
clarinet or saxophone and piano
MS [MGG]

Gerhard, Roberto (Spanish, b. 1896)

Wind Quintet (1928)
MS [MGG]

Seven Hai-Kai (1922)
soprano, winds and piano
    [G5]

Gerster, Ottmar (German, b. 1897)

MGG mentions works (1936) for 5 winds.

Ghedini, Giorgio Fedeice (Italian, b. 1892)

Concerto grosso (1927)
IIII-01 and strings
MS [MGG]

Quintette (1910)
IIII-01
MS [MGG]

Doppio Quintette (1921)
woodwind quintet, 4 strings, harp and piano
MS [MGG]

Concerto a cinque (1930)
1111- and piano
MS [MGG]

Gieseking, Walter (b. 1895, famous French-born German pianist)

Quintet (1920)
111-01 and piano
MS [MGG]

Variations on a Theme of Grieg (1938)
flute and piano
MS [MGG]

Sonatine for flute and piano
MS [MGG]

Ginastera, Alberto (Brasilian, b. 1916)

Impresiones de la Puma (1934)
flute and string quartet
MS [MGG]

Duo (1945)
flute and oboe
MS [MGG]

Glanville-Hicks, Peggy (Australian, b. 1912)

Aria Concertante
tenor female choir, oboe, piano and gong
MS [G5]

Goleminov, Marin (b. 1908)

2 wind quintets (1936, 1946)
MS [MGG]

Goossens, Eugene (English, b. 1893)

Fanfare for a Ceremony (1921)
4 trumpets
MS [G5]

Four Sketches (1912)
flute, violin and piano
MS [MGG]

Suite, Op. 6 (1914)
flute, violin and harp
MS [MGG]

Pastoral and Harlequinade, Op. 41 (1924)
flute, oboe and piano
[MGG]

Grove, Stefans (German, b. 1922)

Trio (1925)
winds
MS [MGG]

Grunewald, Jean-Jacques (French, b. 1911)

Fantasie-Arabesque (1937)
harpsichord, oboe, clarinet and bassoon
(Paris: Salabert)

Guerrini, Guido (Italian, b. 1890)

Canzone e danza (1932)
2 clarinets and 2 bassoons
MS [MGG]

Haba, Alois (Czech, b. 1893)

3 *Nonettes*, Op. 40, 41 and 82 (1931–1935)
wind quintet and 4 strings
MS [MGG]

Quartet, Op. 74 (1951
4 bassoons
MS [MGG]

Haba, Karl (Czech, b. 1898)

Wind quintet, Op. 28 (1945)
MS [MGG]

Harmat, Arthur (Hungarian, b. 1885)

Psalm CL
chorus, organ, 2 trumpets, 2 trombones, timpani
MS [G5]

Harris, Roy (American, b. 1898)

Fantasy (1932)
flute, oboe, clarinet, bassoon, horn and piano
MS [MGG]

4 Minutes - 20 Seconds (1934)
flute and string quartet
MS [MGG]

Harsányi, Tibor (Hungarian, 1898–1954)

Nonette (1927)
wind quintet and 4 strings
MS [MGG]

Haudebert, Lucien (French, b. 1877)

Suite dans le style ancient
wind quartet
MS [MGG]

Haug, Hans (German, b. 1900)

Wind Quartet (1925)
MS [MGG]

Wind Quintet (1955)
MS [MGG]

Hausswald, Gunter (German, b. 1908)

Quintett, Op. 34
clarinet and strings
MP (Breitkopf & Härtel)

Henkemanns, Hans (German, b. 1913)

Quintett (1934)
IIII-OI
MS [MGG]

Hennessy, Swan (French, 1866–1929)

Deux morceaux
saxophone, viola and piano
MP (Paris: M. Eschig, 1926)

Quatre morceaux for saxophone or viola and piano
MP (Paris: Eschig, 1929)

Henriques, Fini Valdimar (Danish, 1867–1940)

Suite, Op. 13 (1894)
oboe and strings
MP (Hansen)

Quartet (1937)
flute, violin, cello and piano
MS [MGG]

Henze, Hans Werner (German, b. 1926)

Kranichsteiner Kammerkonzert (1946)
flute, piano and strings
MS [MGG]

Sonatine
flute and piano
MS [MGG]

Wind quintet (1953)
MS [MGG]

Der Vorwurf (1948), concert aria
baritone, trumpet, trombone and strings
MS [MGG]

Herberigs, Robert (Belgian, b. 1886)

Landelijk Concerto (1937)
wind quintet
MS [MGG]

Sonatine (1952)
flute and strings
MS [MGG]

Miniatursuite (1953)
flute and strings
MS [MGG]

Cyrano de Bergerac (1910)
horn and orchestra
MS [MGG]

Herrmann, Hugo (German, b. 1896)

Romantische Episoden, Op. 13c
wind quintet
MS [MGG]

Kleine Suite, Op. 24a
5 winds
MP (Trossingen: Hohner)

Pastorale Phantasietten, Op. 51
wind quintet
MS [MGG]

Sieben Spielmusiken, Op. 578a
3 winds
MS [MGG]

Chamber cantata
chorus, flute saxophone and string bass
[MGG]

Heseltine, Philip (English, 1894–1930)

The Curlew
tenor, flute, English horn and string quartet
MP (London: Stainer & Bell, 1924)

Hess, Ernst (German, b. 1912)

Concerto, Op. 24, (1943)
horn and orchestra
MS [MGG]

Quintett (1938)
clarinet and strings
MS [MGG]

Quintett (1943)
oboe and strings
MS [MGG]

Hess, Willy (German, b. 1906)

Divertimento, Op. 51
5 winds
MS [MGG]

Hill, Alfred (American, b. 1870)

Miniature Trio, Nr. 1
clarinet or violin, cello and piano
MP (New York: Schirmer)

Miniature Trio, Nr. 2
clarinet or violin, cello and piano
MP (New York: Schirmer)

Hill, Edward Burlingame (b. 1872)

Sextet, Op. 39 (1934)
piano and winds
MP (New York: Society for the Publication of American Music)

Clarinet quintet (1945)
MS [MGG]

Hlobil, Emil (Czech, b. 1901)

Wind Quintet, Op. 20 (1941)
MS [MGG]

Hochreiter, Emil (German, 1871–1938)

Music for 4 Horns (1929)
MS [MGG]

Hoffding, Niels Finn (Danish, b. 1899)

Woodwind Quintet, Op. 35 (1940)
MP (Skandinavisk Musikforlag)

Woodwind Quintet, Nr. 2, Op. 53 (1953)
MP (self-published)

Quartett, Op. 11 (1927)
soprano, oboe, 4-hand piano
MP (self-published)

Höffer, Paul (German, 1895–1949)

Kleine Holzblaser-Suite (1944)
MS [MGG]

Variations über ein thema von Beethoven
wind quintet (1947)
MP (Leipzig: Peters)

Höller, Karl (German, b. 1907)

Hymnen, Op. 13 (1932)
male chorus, 3 trumpets, organ and percussion
MS [MGG]

Clarinet Quintet, Op. 46 (1947)
MS [MGG]

Divertimento, Op. 11 (1931)
flute, viola, cello and piano
MS [MGG]

Holfritz, Hans (Swiss, b. 1902)

Concerto for saxophone and orchestra
MS [MGG]
This score won first prize at a festival in Chile in 1948.

Holmboe, Vagn (Danish, b. 1909)

Notturno, Op. 19 (1940)
woodwind quintet
MP (Kopenhagen: Viking)

Hopkins, Anthony (b. 1921)

The Crown of Gold (1944), cantata
3 soloists, string quartet, Eng. hn and piano
MS [MGG]

Hubeau, Jean (French, b. 1917)

Sonata humoresque (1942)
flute, clarinet, horn and piano
MP (Paris: Noël, 1942)

Huber-Anderach, Theodor (German, b. 1885)

Turmmisol, Op. 45
2 trumpets and 2 trombones
MS [MGG]

Graduale und off. Zum Feste Peter und Paul, Op. 28
chorus, 2 trumpets, trombone
MP (Zurich: Hug)

Huber, Hans (Swiss, 1852–1921)

Quintet in Eb, Op. 136
piano and winds
MP (National-Ausg. Des Schweiz. Tonkünstlerverlag)

Sextett for piano and winds
MP (National-Ausg. Des Schweiz. Tonkünstlerverlag)

Huré, Jean (French, 1877–1930)

Concertstück
saxophone and orchestra
MS [MGG]

Hurnik, Ilja (Czech, b. 1922)

Blaserquintett (1949)
MS [MGG]

Ingenhoven, Jan (Dutch, 1876–1951)

Quintett (1911)
woodwind quintet
MS [MGG]

Kammermusik (1926)
clarinet and string trio
MS [MGG]

Ippisch, Franz (German, b. 1883)

Blaserquintett (1926)
MS [MGG]

Clarinet quintet (1942)
MS [MGG]

Ippolitow Iwanow, Michail Michailowirsch (Russian, 1859–1935)

Ein Abend in Georgien, Op. 69a
flute, oboe, clarinet, bassoon and harp
MS [MGG]

3 kirgisische Lieder (1931)
flute, oboe, clarinet and bassoon
[MGG]

Jachino, Carlo (Italian, b. 1887)

Tre Madrigali (1951)
singer, flute and harp
MS [MGG]

James, Philip (American, b. 1890)

Suite (1936)
woodwind quintet
MP (New York: C. Fischer, 1938)

Járdányi, Pál (Hungarian, b. 1920)

Phantasie u. Var. über ungar. Vld (1955), Hungarian folksongs
wind quintet
MS [MGG]

Jenny, Albert (1912-1992, organist)

Rhapsodie
saxophone and string orchestra (1938)
MS [MGG]

Jeppesen, Knud (German, b. 1892, the great Palestrina scholar)

Domine, refugium factum est (1958), cantata
soprano, flute, violin
MS [MGG]

Jerger, Wilhelm (German, b. 1902)

Es schaut der weite Kreis der Erde, Grad. Ad III. Missam in die Nat. dom., in Freier deutscher, Cantata
soprano, chorus, boys choir, brass and organ
MP (Augsburg: Böhm, 1936)

Jirak, Karle Boleslav (Czech, b. 1891)

Wind quintet, Op. 34 (1928)
MS [MGG]

Jochum, Otto (German, b. 1898)

Der Herzbrunnen, Op. 49 (1933), Serenade
5 winds and 5 strings
MS [MGG]

Blütenzweige vom Mondnachtbaum, Op. 104 (1950)
mezzo-soprano and 2 flutes
MS [MGG]

Goldene Blutenzeif, Op. 117 (1952)
female choir, clarinet and horn
MS [MGG]

Jolivet, André (French, b. 1905)

Suite liturgique (1942)
tenor or soprano, Eng. hn, oboe, cello and harp
MP (Paris: Durand)

Chant de Lino (1944)
flute and piano
MP (Paris: Costallet, 1944)
MP (Paris: Leduc, 1954, the same with flute, strings and harp)

Serenade (1945)
oboe solo and woodwind quintet
MP (Paris: Costallet)

Jones, Charles (American, b. 1910)

Down with Drink (1943)
women's chorus, piano and percussion
MS [G5]

Juon, Paul (Russian, 1872–1940)

Divertimento, Op. 51 (1913)
flute, oboe, clarinet, bassoon, horn and piano

Quintett, Op. 84 (1930)
woodwind quintet
MS [MGG]

Kadosa, Pál (Hungarian, b. 1903)

Sonata Nr. 2, Op. 9 (1927)
wind quartet
MP (Mainz: Schott)

Kallstenius, Edvin, Swedish, b. 1881

Quintet, Op. 17 (1930)
clarinet and string quartet, revised as a wind sextet
MS [MGG]

Wind Quintet, Op. 29 (1943), revised as *Divertimento da camera*, Op. 29b (1848) for orchestra
MS [MGG]

Piccolo trio seriale, Op. 47 (1956)
flute, clarinet and Eng. horn
MS [MGG]

Kardos, Dezider (Slovak, b. 1914)

Dvchové kvintete, (1938)
wind quintet
MS [MGG]

Karg-Elert, Sigfrid (German, 1877–1933)

25 Capricen and Sonatas Op. 153
saxophone
MP (Zimmermann)

Quintett, Op. 30 (1904)
oboe, 2 clarinets, horn and bassoon
MP (Leipzig: Kahnt)

Partita retrospettiva, Op. 139 (1919)
flute, oboe, trumpet and piano
MP [MGG]

Sinfonietta exotica (1921)
3 flutes, bass clarinet and harp
MS [MGG]

Die Grablegung Christi, Op. 84 (1913), a *Choralkanzene*
soprano, oboe, Eng. horn and organ
MP (Leipzig: Breitkopf & Härtel)

Kauffmann, Leo (German, 1901–1944)

Allegro commodo (1930)
4 horns
MS [MGG]

Woodwind Quintett (1943)
MP (Vienna: Universal Edition)

Kayser, Leif (Danish, b. 1919)

Variazioni sopra 'In dulci jubil' (1954)
4 brass
MS [MGG]

Keller, Wilhelm (German, b. 1920)

Uroboros, Tanzspiel (1957)
soli, chorus, dancers, percussion and piano
MP (Munich: Ed. Modern)

Three Songs (1950)
singer and oboe
MS [MGG]

Lied der Freundin (Detmold, 1950)
soprano, flute and harp
MS [MGG]

Kenessey, Jenö (Hungarian, b. 1906)

Quintett (1953)
2 flutes, 2 trumpets and harp
MS [MGG]

Klebe, Giselher (German, b. 1925)

Wind Quintet, Op. 3 (1948)
MS [MGG]

Knorr, Ernst-Lothar von (German, b. 1896)

Sonata
flute, alto saxophone, violin, viola, cello, cembalo and piano
MP (Mainz: Schott)

Koechlin, Charles (French, 1867–1950)

Deux sonatines, Op. 194 (1943)
oboe d'amore or soprano saxophone and chamber orchestra
MS [MGG]

Kókai, Rezzö (Hungarian, b. 1906)

Quartettine (1952)
clarinet and strings
MS [MGG]

Komma, Karl Michael (German, b. 1913)

Divertimento (1957)
flute, oboe, clarinet, horn, bassoon and strings
MS [MGG]

Koppel, Herman David (Danish, b. 1908)

Sextett, Op. 36 (1942)
wind quintet and piano
MP (Kopenhagen: Skandinavisk Musikforlag, 1947)

Sonatine, Op. 16 (1932)
MS [MGG]

Kósa, György (Hungarian, b. 1897)

Szél az Ur, biblische Kantata (1957)
chorus and tuba
MS [MGG]

Furesa rimes játék (1957)
2 female singers, oboe, Eng. hn, bassoon and harp
MS [MGG]

Dies irae (1937)
chorus, organ and percussion
MS [MGG]

Kovarovic, Karl (Czech, 1862–1920)

Duett for clarinet and horn
MS [MGG]

Kraft, Karl Joseph (German, b. 1903)

Divertimento Nr. 1
flute, clarinet and bassoon
MS [MGG]

Divertimento Nr. 2
oboe, Eng. horn and horn
MS [MGG]

Divertimento Nr. 3
flute, oboe and clarinet
MS [MGG]

Holder Morgen (1942)
female choir and 3 winds
MS [MGG]

Krein, Alexander Abemowitsch (1883–1951)

2 *Suiten Jewrejskije eskisy* (Hebrew Sketches) (1910)
clarinet and string quartet
MS [MGG]

Krejcí, Isa (Czech, b. 1904)

Concertino (1936)
piano and winds
MS [G5]

Lieder (1936)
singer and wind quintet
MS [MGG]

Kasace (1925)
flute, clarinet, trumpet and bassoon
[MGG]

Kremenliev, Boris Angeloff (Bulgarian, b. 1911)

Come rain
women's voices and 2 trumpets
MS [MGG]

Kronsteiner, Hermann (German, b. 1914)

Kleine Festmesse (1949)
chorus, organ with 4 winds ad. lib.
MP (Vienna: Doblinger)

Kricka, Jaroslav (b. 1882)

Divertimento, Op. 99 (1950)
wind quintet
MS [MGG]

Kundigraber, Hermann (German, 1879–1944)

Quintet, Op. 1
212-
MS [MGG]

Kunz, Ernst (German, b. 1891)

Quintett (1916)
winds and harp
MS [MGG]

Kvapil, Jaroslav (Czech, 1892–1958)

Quartet (1948)
flute and strings
MS [MGG]

Ladmirault, Paul (French, 1877–1944)

Choral et Variations (1935)
wind quintet and piano
MP (Paris: Lemoine, 1952)

Lahmer, Ruel (American, b. 1912)

Folk Fun (1947)
unison chorus, flute, clarinet and 2 pianos
MS [G5]

Lajtha, László (Hungarian, b. 1892)

Intermezzo Op. 59 (1954)
alto saxophone and piano
MP (Paris: Leduc)

Lamy, Fernand (French, b. 1881)

Sonette (1924) [This is Nr. 4 of *Quatre ballades*]
4 female voices, oboe, Eng. horn, horn and bassoon
MP (Paris: Leduc)

Landowski, Marcel (French, b. 1915)

Trio (1954)
horn, trumpet and piano
MS [MGG]

Landré, Guillaume (Dutch, b. 1905)

Wind quintet (1930)
MS [MGG]

Langlais, Jean (French, b. 1907)

Mass Salve Regina (1954)
2 choirs, 2 organs and brass
MS [MGG]

Larmanjat, Jacques (French, 1878–1952)

2 *Saxophone s*oli (1931), from the film *Entre deux Eaux*
MS [MGG]

Quatre pieces en Concert (1956), for saxophone and piano
MP (Paris: Durand)

Larsson, Lars-Erik (Swedish, b. 1908)

Concerto (1934)
saxophone and string orchestra
MS [MGG]

Lazarus, Daniel (French, b. 1898)

Sonata (1948)
alto saxophone
MP (Paris: Durand)

Legley, Victor (Belgian, b. 1915)

Sonata
trumpet, clarinet and organ
MS [MGG]

Leibowitz, René (French, b. 1913)

Wind quintet, Op. 11 (1958)
MS [MGG]

Leigh, Walter (English, 1905–1942)

Trio (1935)
flute, oboe and piano
MS [MGG]

Lajtha, László (Hungarian, b. 1892)

Intermezzo Op. 59 (1954)
alto saxophone and piano
MP (Paris: Leduc)

Lhotka, Fran (Czech, b. 1883)

Kleine Suite (1928)
4 flutes
MS [MGG]

Pastorale und Scherzo (1949), for wind quintet
MS [MGG]

Liebermann, Rolf (Swiss, b. 1910)

Rondo (1953)
saxophone and piano
MP (Zurich: Universal Edition)

Lier, Betus Van (b. 1906)

Drei alt-pers. Vierzeiler (1956)
soprano, alto flute, oboe d'amore and piano
MS [MGG]

McEwen, John Blackwood (Scottish, 1868–1948)

Under Northern Skies (1939)
woodwind quintet
MS [MGG]

Maasz, Gerhard (German, b. 1906)

Finckenschlag. Var. über Alle Vogel (1952)
IIII-
MP (Sikorski)

Maconchy, Elizabeth (English, b. 1907)

Quintett (1932)
oboe and strings
MS [MGG]

6 Gedichte (1951)
female chorus, clarinet, 2 horns and harp
MS [MGG]

Magnard, Alberic (French, 1856–1914)

Quintette, Op. 8 (1904)
IIII-, piano
MP (Paris: Rouat Lerolle)

Malipiero, Gian Francesco (Italian, 1882–1914)

Sonata a quattre (1954)
flute, oboe, clarinet and bassoon
MP (Vienna: Universal Edition)

Malipiero, Riccardo (Italian, b. 1914)

Dialoghi. Nr. 4 (1956)
woodwind quintet
MP (Milan: Riccordi)

Musica da camera (1959)
woodwind quintet
MS [MGG]

Maros, Rudolf (Hungarian, b. 1917)

Musica leggiera (1956)
woodwind quintet
MP (Budapest: Zenemükiadó Vállalat)

Maric, Ljubica (Yugoslavian, b. 1909)

Woodwind quintet (1932)
MS [MGG]

Marinuzzi, Gino (Italian, b. 1882)

Concertino (1936)
clarinet, oboe, saxophone and strings
MP (Milan: Carisch)

Marsick, Armand-Louis-Joseph (French, 1877–1959)

Quatuor pour quatre cors in fa
MP (Brüssel: Cebedem, 1950)

Marisck, Martin-Pierre-Joseph (French, 1848–1924)

Souvenir de Naples, Op. 35 (1914)
flute, clarinet and string quintet
MP (Paris: Senart)

Martin, Frank (Swiss, b. 1890)

Balade (1938)
saxophone, piano, string orchestra and percussion
MS [MGG]

Martinu, Bohuslav (Czech, 1890–1959)

Pastorale
5 Blockflutes, clarinet, 2 violins and cello
MS [MGG]

Wind Quintet
MS [MGG]

Marx, Karl (German, b. 1897)

Divertimento, Op. 21a (1943)
flute, 4 strings and piano
MS [MGG]

Botschaft, Op. 41 (1941)
soprano, 2 Blockflutes and piano
MS [MGG]

Frühlingstau in deinen Augen, Op. 138 (1939)
alto, Blockflute and piano
MS [MGG]

Meilers, Wilfrid (English, b. 1914)

Lysistrata (1948), a play in music
soprano, baritone, speaking chorus, flute, oboe, clarinet, bassoon, trumpet, string bass
    and percussion
MS [G5]

News from Greece (1949)
mezzo-soprano, chorus, 3 trumpets, percussion and 2 pianos
MS [G5]

Migot, Georges (French, b. 1891, Superintendent of the Instrument Collection of the Paris Conservatory)

La Mise au tombeau (1949)
small chorus and wind quintet
MS [MGG]

Wind Quintet (1954)
MS [MGG]

Quatuor (1955)
saxophones
MS [MGG]

McPhee, Colin (American, b. 1901)

Sonatina (1925)
2 flutes, clarinet, trumpet and piano
MS [MGG]

The Revelation of St. John the Divine (1935)
male chorus, 3 trumpets, 2 pianos and timpani
MS [MGG]

Meester, Louis de (Belgian, b. 1904)

Divertimento (1946)
wind quartet
MS [MGG]

Melartia, Erkki (Finnish, 1857–1937)

2 *Wind quartets*
MS [MGG]

Merikanto, Frans Oskar (Finnish, 1868–1924)

Partita
2121-, harp
MS [MGG]

Meulemans, Arthur (Belgium, b. 1884)

2 *Bläser-Quintette*
MS [MGG]

Moeshinger, Albert (Swiss, b. 1897)

Visions du Moyen-âge, Op. 52
tenor, clarinet and string orchestra
MS [MGG]

Image, Op. 85
flute, saxophone, violin and cello
MS [MGG]

Mohler, Phillpp (German, b. 1908)

Vergangen is die Nacht, Op. 14 (Nürnberg)
female chorus, flute and string orchestra
MP (Mainz: Schott, 1943)

Mohr, Wilhelm (German, b. 1904)

Bläserquintett, Op. 6 (Hamburg), 1943
Variations über das Lied vom Heuschreck
wind quintet or string quintet
MP (Munich: Kasparek)

Molnár, Antal (Hungarian, b. 1890)

Jazz Satire (1928)
small jazz ensemble
MS [MGG]

Monnikendam, Marius (Dutch, b. 1896)

Missa Festiva
chorus, 2 trumpets, 2 trombones and organ
MP (Utrecht: Van Rossum, 1955)

Concerto (1958)
4 brass and organ
MS [MGG]

Moore, Douglas (American, b. 1893)

Ballade of William Sycamore (1926)
baritone singer, flute, trombone and piano
MS [MGG]

Woodwind Quintet (1942)
MP (New York: G. Schirmer, 1948)

Clarinet Quintet (1946)
MS [MGG]

Moritz, Edvard (German, b. 1891)

3 *Quintets for winds,* Op. 25
MS [MGG]

Moser, Franz (Austrian, 1880–1939)

Nocturne, Op. 64
oboe, clarinet, horn, bassoon and piano
MS A:Wn (Sm 21281)

Capriccio, Op. 64, Nr. 2
oboe, clarinet, horn bassoon and piano

Zwei Impressonen, Op. 66, Nr. 1
flute, oboe, clarinet, bassoon, and piano; with Nr. 2 for flutes (with piccolo), oboe (with
    Eng. horn) clarinet, bassoon and piano
MS A:Wn (Sm 21286)

Grotesken in Perpetenmobile
flute, oboe, clarinet, bassoon and piano
MS A:WN (Sm 21302)

Trio, Op. 38 (1923)
2 oboes, Eng. horn
MS A:Wn (Sm 21203)

2 *Stücke*, Op. 76a, 76b
5 horns
MS A:Wn (Sm 21314)

Moyzes, Mikulás (Slovakian, 1872–1944)

Wind quintet (1935)
    [MGG]

Müller, Paul (German, b. 1898)

Choraltoccata über 'Ein fest Burg,' Op. 54, Nr. 1
2 trumpets and 2 trombones
MS [MGG]

Choralfantasie über 'Wie schön leuchtet der Morgenstern,' Op. 52, Nr. 2 (1955)
2 trumpets and 2 trombones
MS [MGG]

Choralfantasie über 'Ach Gott von Himmel sieh darein,' Op. 56 (1955)
2 trumpets and 2 trombones
MS [MGG]

Choralfantasie über 'Christ ist erstanden,' (1957)
2 trumpets, trombone
MS [MGG]

Muñez, Melleda, Jose (b. 1905)

Divertimento (1944)
piccolo, flute, oboe, clarinet, bassoon and trumpet
MS [MGG]

Nielsen, Carl August (Danish, 1865–1931)

Quintet, Op. 43 (1922)
winds
MS [MGG]

Nigg, Serge (French, b. 1924)

Suite (1955)
flute, 4 strings and harp
MP (Paris: Sofirad, 1955)

Niverd, Lucien (French, b. 1879)

Crepuscule d'automne
horn or saxophone and piano
MP (Nizza: Delrieu, 1951)

Oboussier, Robert (German, 1900–1957)

3 *Arien nach Klopstock* (1936)
coloratura soprano, oboe and cembalo
MS [MGG]

Olsen, Carl Gustav (Danish, b. 1903)

Woodwind quintet, Op. 35
MP (Kopenhagen: Iyche)

Osterc, Slavko (Slovakian, 1895–1941)

Quintett (1932)
winds
MS [MGG]

Sonata (1935) for saxophone and piano
MS [MGG]

Ave Maria (1930)
soprano, alto, oboe, saxophone and clarinet
MS [MGG]

Othegraven, August von (German, 1864–1946)

Advent, Op. 70, cantata
soprano chorus, 2 trumpets, 3 trombones, timpani and organ
MS (Leipzig: Leuckart, 1927)

Pahissa, Jaime (Spanish, b. 1880)

Dos canciones del campo (1955)
wind quintet
MS [MGG]

Palmer, Robert (American, b. 1915)

Wind quintet (1951)
MS [MGG]

Panufnik, Tomasz (Polish, 1876–1951)

Quintet for winds (1953)
MS (Poln. Musikverlag, 1954)

Papandopulo, Boris (Croatian, b. 1906)

Quintett, Op. 90 (1940)
clarinet and string quartet
MP (Agram: Savez kompozitora Joguslavije, 1960)

Pâque, M. J. L. Désiré (French, 1867–1939)

Petite Suite, Op. 40
flute, clarinet, oboe and piano
MS [MGG]

Trois courtes pieces, Op. 131 (1936)
4 horns
MS [MGG]

Parrott, Ian (English, b. 1916)

Wind quintet (1948)
Scherzo (1951)
oboe, oboe d'amore, Eng. horn, Heckelphone
MS   [MGG]

Peeters, Emil (Dutch, b. 1893)

Wind quintet (1953)
MS   [MGG]

Peeters, Flor (Belgian, b. 1903)

Suite (1955)
trombone quartet
MP   (Peters, 1960)

Entrata Festiva (1959)
2 trumpets, 2 trombones and timpani
MP   (Peters, 1959)

Choralfantasy on 'Christ the Lord has risen'
2 trumpets, 2 trombones and organ
MP   (Gray, 1961)

Pepping, Ernst (German, b. 1901)

Suite (1925), Donaueschingen
trumpet, alto saxophone and trombone

Perosi, Lorenzo (Italian, 1872-1956)

MGG attributes to Perosi 200 compositions for clarinet and piano.

Petrzelka, Vilém (Moravian, b. 1889)

Miniatuy [Miniatures], Op. 54
wind quintet
MS   [MGG]

Picha, Frantisek (Czech, b. 1893)

Wind quintet, Op. 31 (1943)
MS   [MGG]

Pijper, Willem (Dutch, 1894–1947)

Woodwind quintet (1929)
MS [MGG]

Sextet (1923)
woodwind quintet and piano
MS [MGG]

Polivka, Vladimir (Czech, 1896–1948)

Suite (1933)
viola and wind quintet
MS [MGG]

Poot, Marcel (Dutch, b. 1901)

Quintet for winds, 1959
MS [MGG]

Porter, Quincy (American, b. 1897)

Divertimento
wind quintet
MP (New York: Peters, 1962)

Poston, Elisabeth (English, b. 1905)

Sonatina
winds and piano (1951)
MS [MGG]

Pujol, Francisco (1878–1945)

Himne dels nois
singer, oboe, Eng. horn and harp
MS [MGG]

Quef, Charles (French, 1873–1931)

Suite, Op. 4 (1902)
winds and piano
MS [MGG]

Ranki, Gyorgy (Hungarian, b. 1907)

Quintet (1929)
oboe, clarinet, bassoon, horn and piano
MS [MGG]

Pentaerophonia (1958), three works
woodwind quintet
MS [MGG]

Raphael, Gunter (German, 1903–1960)

Quartet, Op. 61 (1945)
flute, oboe, clarinet and bassoon
MP (Heidelberg: Müller)

Quintett, Op. 4 (1924)
clarinet and strings
MP (Berlin: Simrock)

Divertimento, Op. 74 (1952)
saxophone and cello
MS [MGG]

Recitatif (1958)
saxophone and piano
MP (Paris: Leduc)

Sonata (1957)
saxophone and piano
MS [MGG]

Rathaus, Karol (Hungarian, 1895–1954)

Kleine Serenade, Op. 23 (1927)
clarinet, bassoon, horn, trumpet and piano
MS [MGG]

Reichel, Bernard (Swiss, b. 1901)

Octuor (1938)
2 violins, viola, string bass, saxophone, trumpet and piano
MS [MGG]

Prelude, Passacaille et Postlude (1951)
woodwind quintet
MS [MGG]

EARLY TWENTIETH-CENTURY REPERTOIRE FOR FIVE OR FEWER WIND PLAYERS   169

Reizenstein, Franz (English, b. 1911)

Wind quintet, Op. 5 (1934)
MS [MGG]

Theme, Variations & Fugue, Op. 2 (1960)
clarinet and string quartet
MS [MGG]

Reuter, Fritz (German, b. 1896)

Suite for trombone alone
MS [MGG]

Riegger, Wallingford (American, b. 1885)

Eternity (1942)
female chorus, flutes, 2 horns and bass
MS [G5]

Rieti, Vittorio (Italian, b. 1898)

Concerto for 5 woodwinds (1923)
MP (Vienna: Universal Edition, 1924)

Concertino (1935)
5 clarinets

Sonata (Vienna, 1925)
flute, oboe, bassoon and piano

Partita
cembalo, flute, oboe and string quartet
MP (New York: Broude)

Riisager, Knudage (Danish, b. 1887)

2 Wind quintets (1921, 1927)
MS [MGG]

Wind quartet (1941)
MS [MGG]

Concertino (1932
oboe, clarinet, bassoon
MS [MGG]

Petite Suite (1932)
flute, 2 clarinets and bassoon
    [MGG]

Divertimento (1944)
flute, oboe, bassoon and horn
    [MGG]

Ristic, Milan (Polish, b. 1908)

Wind quintet (1936)
MS [MGG]

Suite (1938)
4 trombones
MS [MGG]

Rivier, Jean (French, b. 1896)

Concerto (1954)
saxophone, trumpet and strings
MP (Paris: P. Noël)

Rocca, Lodovico (Italian, b. 1895)

Storiella
2 trumpets, bassoon, harp and piano
MP (Milan: Riccordi, 1940)

Röder, Carl, (Austrian, nineteenth century)

Fantasie
bassoon and piano
MS A:Gmf (VIII 30642)

Concertino
bassoon and orchestra or piano
MS A:Gmf (VIII 30643)

Variations
bassoon and piano
MS A:Gmf (VIII 30644)

Concerto
bassoon and piano
MS A:Gmf (VIII 30645)

Fantasie
bassoon and piano
MS A:Gmf (VIII 30646)

Elegie
bassoon and piano [in memory of H. W. Ernst]
MS A:Gmf (VIII 30648)

Rogister, Jean (Belgium, b. 1879)

Quintette for winds
MS [MGG]

Quartet
flute, viola, cello and harp
MS [MGG]

Dialogue des pedants
clarinet and bassoon
MS [MGG]

Rogowski, Ludomir (Polish, b. 1881)

Piesni mozra [Sea Shanties] (1940)
baritone, 2 horns and piano
MS [G5]

Rohwer, Jens (German, b. 1914)

Quartet
flute, violin, viola and cello
MS [MGG]

Trio
oboe, violin and viola
MS [MGG]

Lieder
singer, clarinet and timpani
    [MGG]

Roldán, Amadeo (Cuban, 1900–1939)

4 Ritmicas
flute, oboe, clarinet, bassoon, trumpet and piano
MS [MGG]

Rootham, Daniel Wilberforce (English, 1837–1922)

Septett
viola, harp and woodwind quintet
MS [MGG]

Rosenberg, Hilding (Swedish, b. 1892)

Wind quintet (1959)
MS [MGG]

Rosenthal, Manuel (French, b. 1904)

Saxophone-Marmelade (1929)
alto saxophone and piano
MS [MGG]

Rosseau, Norbert (Belgian, b. 1907)

Wind quintet, Op. 54 (1955)
MS [MGG]

Roussel, Albert (French, 1869–1937)

Divertissement, Op. 6 (1906)
flute, oboe, clarinet, bassoon, horn and piano
MS [MGG]

Ruyneman, Daniel (Dutch, b. 1886)

Nightingales, Quintet for winds (Amsterdam, 1949)
MS [MGG]

Sachesse, Hans (German, 1891–1960)

Wind Quintet, Op. 32
MP (Augsburg: Böhme)

Serenade, Op. 13
male chorus, soprano, 4 woodwinds and lute
MP (Zurich: Hug)

Saikkola, Lauri (b. 1906)

Divertimento for wind quintet (1952)
MS [MGG]

Salzedo, Carlos (French harpist, 1885–1961)

3 Poems (1919)
soprano, 6 harps and 3 woodwinds
MS [MGG]

Santoliquido, Francesco (Italian, b. 1883)

2 Wind Quintets
MS [MGG]

Sauguet, Henri (French, b. 1901)

Divertissement (1931)
flute, clarinet, viola, bassoon and piano
MS [MGG]

Golden Suite (1963)
2 trumpets, trombone, horn and tuba
MS [MGG]

Schaefer, Theodor (Czech, b. 1904)

Wind quintet, Op. 5 (1935)
MS [MGG]

Divertimento mesto, Op. 22 (1946)
woodwind quintet, 3 strings
MS [MGG]

Schäfer, Karl (German, b. 1899)

Musik über einen Choral (1929)
soprano, 2 trumpets, and organ
MP (Heidelberg: Müller)

Quintett (1930)
clarinet and strings
MS [MGG]

Schelb, Josef (German, b. 1894)

Sextet
flute, clarinet and string quartet
MS [MGG]

Wind quintet
MS [MGG]

Schmid, Heinrich Kaspar (German, 1874–1953)

Woodwind Quintett, Op. 28
MP (Schott)

Schoeck, Othmar (Swiss, b. 1886)

Wanderspuche, on poems of Eichendorff, Op. 42 (1928)
high voice, clarinet, horn, percussion and piano
MS [MGG]

Schouwman, Hans (Dutch, b. 1902)

Old Netherland Christmas Songs, Op. 6
oboe and harp
MS [G5]

3 *Songs*, Op. 31
soprano and wind quintet
MS [G5]

3 *Old Dutch Songs*, Op. 40
high voice and wind quintet
MS [G5]

Schreck, Gustav Ernst (German, 1849–1918)

Nonett
woodwind quintet and 4 strings
MS [MGG]

Begrussung des Meeres, Op. 10
male chorus, 2 horns, and piano 4-hand
MP (Leipzig: Kistner)

'*Gott rückt als Kreigheld in das Feld,*' Cantata, Op. 47
soprano, chorus, trumpet and organ
MS [MGG]

Schroeder, Hermann (German, b. 1904)

Sextet (1957)
winds and piano
MS [MGG]

Schulthess, Walter (Swiss, 1894–1956)

Buddha Gautama
speaker, small chorus, 2 clarinets, flute and percussion
MS [MGG]

Schultz, Svend (Danish, b. 1913)

3 Songs
soprano, flute and piano
MS [G5]

Quartet (1960)
flute and 3 strings
MS [G5]

Schwarz-Schilling, Reinhard (b. 1904)

Variations on a theme of Padre Martini (1926)
oboe, clarinet, horn, bassoon and piano
MS [MGG]

Scontrino, Antonia (Italian, 1850–1922)

Bozzetto, six works
clarinet and piano
MP (Florence: Brizzi and Nicolai, 1909)

Scott, Cyril (English, b. 1879)

Idyll (1923)
voice and flute
MS [G5]

Quintett, Op. 6 (1945)
bassoon and strings
MS [MGG]

Scouris, André (French, b. 1899)

Choral, Marche et Galop (1925)
2 trumpets and 2 trombones
MS [MGG]

Sehlbach, Erich (German, b. 1898)

Wind quintet
MS [MGG]

Wind quartet
MS [MGG]

Seiber, Mátyás (Hungarian, 1905–1960)

Serenade (1925)
2 clarinets, 2 bassoons and 2 horns
MS [MGG]

Fantasy (1945)
flute, horn and string quintet
MP (Milan: S. Zerboni, 1956)

Permutazioni a cinque (1958)
wind quintet
MP (Schott, 1959)

Two Jazzolettes (1929)
2 saxophones, trumpet, trombone, piano and percussion
MS [G5]

Sekles, Bernhard (German, 1872–1934)

Serenade, Op. 14
woodwind quintet, string quartet, string bass and harp
MP (Leipzig: Rahter)

Serocki, Kazimierz (Polish, b. 1923)

Concerto (1953)
trombone and orchestra
MS [MGG]

Suite (1953)
4 trombones
MS [MGG]

Sonatine (1954
trombone and piano
MS [MGG]

Siklós, Albert (Hungarian, 1878–1942)

Quartet Michelangelo
piano, clarinet, bassoon and horn
MS [MGG]

Skalkotas, Nico (Greek, 1904–1949)

Scherzo
piano, oboe, bassoon, trumpet
MS [G5]

Somervell, Arthur (English, 1863–1937)

Quintet (1913)
clarinet and strings
MS [MGG]

Scouris, André (French, b. 1899)

Choral, Marche et Galop (1925
2 trumpets and 2 trombones
MS [MGG]

Sowerby, Leo (American, b. 1895)

2 Woodwind quintets
MS [MGG]

Spisak, Michal (Polish, b. 1914)

Woodwind quintet (1948)
MS [MGG]

Quartet (1938)
oboe, 2 clarinets and bassoon
MS [MGG]

Sprongl, Norbert (Austrian, b. 1892)

Woodwind quintet, Op. 90
MP (Vienna: Doblinger)

Sramek, Vladimir (Czech, b. 1923)

Suite
2 clarinets, bassoon, trumpet and accordion
MS [MGG]

5 Wind quintets (1951–1961)
MS [MGG]

Gitanjali (on Tagore)
speaker and flute
MS [MGG]

Staempfli, Edward (Swiss, b. 1908)

Wind quintet (1934)
MS [MGG]

Konzertante (1947)
2 clarinets, 2 trumpets and timpani
     [MGG]

Quartett (1932)
flute and strings
MS [MGG]

Stanford, Charles Villiers (English, 1852–1924)

Sonata, Op. 129
clarinet and piano
MS [MGG]

Sternberg, Erich-Walter (German, b. 1891)

Wind quintet
MS [MGG]

Stevens, Bernard (English, b. 1916)

Two Fanfares, Op. 12 (1950)
4 natural trumpets
MS [G5]

Stockhausen, Karlheinz (German, b. 1928)

Zeitmasse (Paris, 1956)
5 woodwinds
MS [MGG]

Strastegier, Herman (German, b. 1912)

4 Marienantiphons (1939)
4 singers, 3 woodwinds and organ
MS [MGG]

Striegler, Kurt (German, 1886–1958)

Sextett, Op. 58
woodwind quintet and piano
[MGG]

Kleine Festsuite, Op. 59
4 horns
MS [MGG]

Studer, Hans (Swiss, b. 1911)

Gelobet seist du, Herr (1958)
bass, chorus, flute, oboe and organ
MS [MGG]

Der ire Spielmann (1956
tenor, horn and piano
MS [MGG]

Lieder-folge nach altchin. Gedichten (1961)
soprano, flute, oboe, clarinet and bassoon
MS [MGG]

Sturzenegger, Richard (Swiss, b. 1905)

Die Troerinnen (Euripides/Werfel), Bühnenmusik (1946
5 winds and percussion
MS [MGG]

Suter, Robert (Swiss, b. 1919)

Lyrische Suite (1959)
1110-01 and string orchestra
MS [MGG]

Sutermeister, Heinrich (Swiss, b. 1910)

Serenade Nr. 1 (1949)
21-1
MP (Mainz: Schott)

Serenade Nr. 2 (1961)
1111-11
MP (Mainz: Schott)

Szalowski, Bonifacy (French, 1867–1923)

Concerto (1958)
oboe, clarinet and orchestra without woodwinds
MP (Paris: Edition Française de Musique)

Quintett (1954)
wind instruments
MP (New York: Omega Music Edition)

Székely, Endre (b. 1912)

2 *Wind quintets* (1952, 1961)
MS [MGG]

Szeligowski, Tadeusz (Polish, 1896–1963)

Woodwind quintet (1950)
MP (Krakkau: PWM, 1956)

Szervánszky, Endré (b. 1911)

2 *Wind quintets* (1951, 1957)
[MGG]

Takáscs, Jenö (Hungarian, b. 1902)

Wind quintet
MP (Vienna: Doblinger)

Tardos, Béla (Hungarian, b. 1910)

Quartet (1963)
flute, oboe, clarinet and bassoon
MS [MGG]

Tate Phyllis (English, b. 1911)

Concerto (1944)
saxophone and string orchestra
MS [MGG]

Therstapen, Hans Joachim (German, 1905–1950)

Divertimento, Op. 19 (1931)
5 winds
MS [MGG]

2 *Nachtlieder* (Rilke), Op. 7 (1928)
soprano, flute and piano
MS [MGG]

Thilman, Johannes Paul (German, b. 1906)

Wind quintet, Op. 44a
MS [MGG]

Die 4-Hörner-Musik
MS [MGG]

Thiriet, André (French, b. 1906)

Concerto
clarinet, cello, saxophone, bassoon and timpani
MS [MGG]

4 *Quartets* for winds
MS [MGG]

Quintet for winds
MS [MGG]

Thiriet, Maurice (French, b. 1906)

Les Chemins épuisés [4 Mélodies]
wind quintet or piano
MS [MGG]

Thomson, Vigil (American, b. 1896)

Five Portraits (1929)
4 clarinets
MS [G5]

Tiessen, Heinz (German, b. 1887)

Divertimento, Op. 51 (1942)
5 winds
MS [MGG]

Tomasi, Henri (French, b. 1901)

Concerto
flute, oboe, clarinet, bassoon, alto saxophone and chamber orchestra
MP (Paris: Leduc)

Tovey, Donald (English, 1875–1940)

Divertimento (1899)
oboe and piano
MS [MGG]

Trio, Op. 8 ('style tragique')
clarinet, horn and piano
MS [MGG]

Sonata, Op. 16 (1900)
clarinet and piano
MS [MGG]

Trojan, Václav (Czech, b. 1907)

Dechovy kyintet (wind quintet, 1937)
MP (Prag: SNKLHU, 1956) score

Tscherepnin, Nikolai Nikolajewitsch (Russian, 1873–1945)

MGG attributes to Tscherepnin 30 works for winds and piano.

Valen, Fartein (Norway, 1887–1952)

Serenade, Op. 42 (1947)
woodwind quintet
MS [MGG]

Vaubourgoin, Sohn Mare (France, b. 1907)

6 *Stücke* for saxophone, viola and orchestra
MS [MGG]

Wind quintet (1932)
MS [MGG]

Vellones, Pierre (French, 1889–1939)

Cinq poemes (1930)
singer, 4 harps, 2 saxophones and string bass
MP (Paris: Lemoine)

Rastelli (1937)
saxophone quartet, piano and orchestra
MP (Paris: Lemoine)

Concerto, Op. 65 (1961)
alto saxophone and orchestra
MP (Paris: Lemoine)

Rapsodie, Op. 29 (1949)
alto saxophone, harp, celesta and percussion
MP (Paris: Lemoine)

Cavaliers andalous (1960)
saxophone quartet
MP (Paris: Lemoine)

Vignati, Milos (Czech, 1897–1966)

Wind quintet, Op. 17
MS [MGG]

Villa-Lobos, Heitor (Brazil, 1887–1959)

Ballet: Dansa da terra (1939)
children's chorus and timpani
MS [MGG, G5]

Ballet: Regosijo de uma raca (1937)
solo voices, children chorus, chorus and timpani
MS [MGG, G5]

Nonet
chorus, flute, oboe, clarinet, saxophone, bassoon, celesta, harp and timpani
MS [MGG, G5]

Wind quintet (1928)
MS [MGG, G5]

Vogel, Vladimir (Russo-German, b. 1896)

Oratorio, 'Wagaus Untergang durch die Eitelkeit' (1930)
solo voices, chorus and 5 saxophones
MS [G5]

Dal Quaderno di Francine settenne (1952)
soprano, flute and piano
MP (Milan: Suvini Zerboni)

Volbach, Fritz (German, 1861–1940)

Quintett, Op. 24,
oboes, clarinet, horn, bassoon and piano
MP (Leipzig: Breitkopf & Härtel, 1902)

Vuataz, Roger (b. 1898)

Destin. Symphonie à trois (1954)
alto saxophone, harp and percussion
MS [MGG]

Musique
5 winds (1937)
MS [MGG]

Vuckovic, Vojislav (Yugoslav, 1910–1942)

Two Songs
soprano, oboe, clarinet and bassoon
MP (Belgrad: Ed. Coll., 1938)

Wagner, Siegfried Richard (German, son to the composer, 1869–1930)

Konzert-Stück (1913, Bayreuth)
flute and orchestra
MS [MGG]

Weber, Ludwig (German, 1891–1947)

Wind quintet (1923)
MS [MGG]

Wehrli, Werner (Swiss, 1892–1944)

Allerseele (1932), cantata
solo voice, female choir, 2 trumpets and piano
MS [G5]

Weinzsweig, John (Canadian, b. 1913)

Woodwind quintet (1964)
MS [MGG]

Weis, Flemming (Danish, b. 1898)

Theme and Variations (1945)
woodwind quintet

Serenade uden reelle Hensigter (1937)
woodwind quintet
MP (Kopenhagen: Hansen)

Weismann, Julius (German, 1879–1950)

Concerto, Op. 106 (1930)
flute, clarinet, bassoon, trumpet, timpani and string orchestra
MS [MGG]

Divertimento, Op. 38 (1910)
clarinet, bassoon, horn and piano
MS [MGG]

Variations, Op. 120 (1936)
4 horns
MS [MGG]

Weissensteiner, Raimund (Austrian, b. 1905)

Saxophonsextett (1954)
saxophone and strings
MS [MGG]

Konzert-Suite (1955)
alto saxophone and string orchestra
MS [MGG]

Wellesz, Egon (Austrian, b. 1885)

Suite, Op. 73
oboe, clarinet, horn and bassoon
MP (Sikorski)

Wenzel, Eberhard (German, b. 1896)

Choralkantata, 'Nun freut euch, lieben Christen gemein' (1960)
chorus, 3 winds and organ
MS [MGG]

Whittaker, William Gillies (English, 1876–1944)

Divertimento (1944)
woodwind quintet
MS [MGG]

Four short pieces (1940)
woodwind quintet
MS [MGG]

Wirth, Helmut (German, b. 1912)

Kleine Clementiade
5 winds
MP (Sikorski)

Heiteres Spiel (1937)
5 winds
MS [MGG]

Wittelsbach, Rudolf (b. 1902)

Quartet (1931)
clarinet, trumpet, bassoon and piano
MS [MGG]

Woestijne, David van de (Belgian, b. 1915)

Variations (1965)
2 guitars, flute, oboe, clarinet, bassoon and horn
MS [MGG]

Wohlfahrt, Frank (German, b. 1894)

Festliche Fanfarenmusik (1958)
2 trumpets and 2 trombones
[MGG]

Wood, Ralph (b. 1901)

Concerto (1962)
wind quintet and orchestra
MS [MGG]

Woyrsch, Felix (German, 1860–1944)

Es ist ein Schnitter, Op. 58
4 trombones
MS [MGG]

Woytowicz, Boleslaw (Polish, b. 1899)

Kolysanka (Cradle Song, 1930)
soprano, flute, clarinet, bassoon and harp
MS [MGG, G5]

Wynne, David (Welsh, b. 1900)

Suite (1959)
2 trumpets, 2 trombones
MS [MGG]

Zender, Hans (German, b. 1936)

Saxophone Concerto (1952)
MP (Breitkopf & Härtel)

Wind quintet (1950)
Wind quartet (1957)
MS [MGG]

Zillig, Winfried (German, 1905–1963)

Lustspielsuite (1934)
wind quintet
MS [MGG]

Zöllner, Richard (German, b. 1896)

Wind quartet (Halle, 1927)
MS [MGG]

Wind quintet (1924, Donaueschingen)
clarinet, 2 violins and 2 celli
MS [MGG]

Repertoire in Private Collections

IN THIS CHAPTER I bring to the attention of the reader several important private collections, some of which were introduced to me by correspondents who shared my desire to identify a broader base of artistic repertoire for wind ensembles and bands. In addition, several of these collections are in need of extended study.

REPERTOIRE OF THE CURTIS INSTITUTE WIND ENSEMBLE

Perhaps few readers are aware that there was an important university-level wind ensemble which gave concerts, commissioned music and made recordings more than a decade earlier than the Eastman Wind Ensemble. This early wind ensemble was composed by students of the Curtis Institute of Music in Philadelphia, whose professors included all the principals of the Philadelphia Orchestra. In addition to this student ensemble composed of instrumentalists who would become the most distinguished instrumentalists of the twentieth century their conductor was none other than the great French musician, Marcel Tabeteau, principal oboist of the Philadelphia Orchestra. Tabeteau, apart from being a great musician and oboist, was a very forceful personality and I have had older members of the orchestra tell me that the orchestra itself gave more credit for the accomplishments of this great orchestra to Tabeteau than to Stokowski and Ormandy.

Under Tabuteau as conductor, the Curtis Wind Ensemble performed in public, on radio and made at least one commercial recording, a copy of which I have. A correspondent, Michael Finkelman, the definitive authority on the English horn, wrote of this ensemble,

> The legendary Marcel Tabuteau, during his many years as professor at Curtis, had a wind ensemble under his direction, consisting of the senior students at the place. Many of these then young artists went on to become major names in the symphony world. Furthermore, this group participated in many a broadcast over CBS radio in the great days of American radio. I wonder if any studio discs were cut of these performances?! (CBS did not at that time own Columbia records, incidentally.) There is at least one recording of this ensemble, playing a *Prélude et Fugue* by Pierné, on Victor 4332. One wonders what else there may on disc from this group, which existed for numerous years, with ever-changing personnel.

Finkelman once visited the Curtis library when researching the works of the composer William Strasser (1875–1944). Strasser also composed and arranged for the Curtis Wind Ensemble and Finkelman was able to identify the following works associated with him and the ensemble.

Strasser, William (American, 1875–1944)

Allegro Moderato
1122-12, Eng. hn and basset hn.
MS US:PHci

Baccanale (1940)
2233-04, piccolo, Eng. hn, contrabsn, timpani and percussion
MS US:PHci (M1050/S897/23959)

Concerto (1941)
2243-04, piccolo, Eng. hn, contrabsn, timpani and percussion
MS US:PHci (M.1050/S894/24136/C)

Flute Concerto
2232-04, piccolo, Eng. hn, contrabsn and timpani
MS US:PHci (M1020/S897/12969/C)

Fuga (1940)
2232-04, piccolo, Eng. hn and contrabsn
MS US:PHci (M1050/S897/23739/C)

Mosaics (1936)
3232-02, Eng. hn, bass clarinet
MS US:PHci (M1050/S897/22325/C)

Petenera (Spanish scene, 1940)
2232-04, piccolo, Eng. hn, contrabsn, tamberine and castanets
MS US:PHci (M1050/S897/23810/C)

Prelude and Fugue (1940)
2232-04, piccolo, English hn, contrabsn
MS US:PHci

Three 16th Century Pieces (arr.)
woodwinds and horns
MS US:PHci

Albeniz, Enrique (twentieth century Spanish composer)

Orientale, arr. Strasser
woodwinds and horns
MS US:PHci

Bach, J. S.

Passacaglia in C minor, arr. Strasser
3333, Eng. hn, bass clarinet, contrabsn
MS US:PHci (M1050/B118/21799/C)

Prelude & Fugue in C, arr. Strasser (1935)
3243, Eng. hn, bass clarinet, contrabsn
    US:PHci
    A performance of this work on April 9, 1936, Tabuteau conducting, included student members: Julius Baker, flute; Rhadames Angelucci and Harry Schulman, oboes and Manny Zegler, bassoon.

Franck, César (French, 1822–1890)

Panis Angelicus, arr. Strasser
1122-02, Eng. hn, bass clarinet
MS US:PHci (M1050/F822/22886/C)

Isaac (Renaissance composer)

Love Song
122-01, Eng. hn, bass clarinet
MS US:PHci (M759/173/23082)

Turina, Joaquin (Spanish, 1882–1949), arr. Strasser

Coins de Séville
woodwinds, harp and percussion
MS US:PHci

Femms d'Espagne
1121-02, piccolo, Eng. hn, bass clarinet, contrabsn
MS US:PHci (M1050/T938/23589)

I might add that the many French associations which Tabuteau shared with the earlier great oboist of the Boston Symphony Orchestra, Georges Longy, makes it reasonable to suppose that the idea for the Curtis Wind Ensemble was founded in imitation of the earlier Longy Club, a professional wind ensemble in Boston consisting of members of that orchestra. This association seems strengthened by the fact that the daughter of Longy, Renée Longy Miquelle, taught solfége at Curtis from 1926–1941. Further, on or about 1929, a portion of the original Longy Club library was deposited in the Curtis library.

Of these compositions associated with the Longy Club which can still be found in the Curtis Institute Library, five are in the hand of the copyist Léon Duclos, rue Chaptal 20, Paris, and the remaining one, the *Quintet* by Strube, appears to be in the hand of a German violinist living in Boston after 1894, Gustav Strube.

Wailly, Paul de (French, fl. 1882–1900)

Ottetto
1122-11
MS US:PHci

Malherbe, Edmond (French, 1870–1963)

Sextuor
1111-01 and Eng. hn
MS US:PHci

LaCroix, Eugene (French, nineteenth century)

Sextuor
1111-01, piano
MS US:PHci

Strube, Gustav (nineteenth century German violinist living in Boston)

Quintet
1111-01
MS US:PHci

Enesco, Georges (Romanian composer)

Dixtuor
2122-02, Eng. hn
MS US:PHci
  The score and parts have stickers reading, 'Longy-Club.'

Caplet, André (French composer)

Suite persane
2222-02
MS US:PHci

I am confident the reader can see that not only this repertoire is very worthy of study but also a study of the Curtis Institute Wind Ensemble itself, in all of its activities.

THE CHERYL BISHKOFF COLLECTION IN NEWBURGH, NY

Some years ago it was my pleasure to have a brief communication with Mary Lenom, the widow of one of the members of the Longy Club wind ensemble of Boston. She was already very elderly and unable to climb the stairs of her large home in order to satisfy my curiosity regarding remaining portions of the Longy Club library which she might still have. But she knew that she had at this time the complete library of her husband, the oboist Clement Lenom, including manuscript recollections of lessons with him collected by a student.

The fact that she was a 'very dear friend' of Longy's daughter, Renée, and had visited the widow of Longy at their retirement home near Abbeville, France, raised my hopes that she may have some of the Longy library. After her passing, Michael Finkelman was able to visit her daughter Cherl Bishkoff, of Newburgh, NY, where he found a substantial wind library, including works with the Longy library stamp.

Alkan [pseudonym for Charles Morhange] (1813–1888)

Marcia funèbre sulla Morte d'un Papagallo
4 voices, 3 oboes, bassoon
MP (Paris: Costallant)

Boisdeffre, René (1838–1906)

'Scherzo' from the *Septuor*, Op. 49
MP (Paris: Hamelle)

Brun, ? (French, nineteenth century)

Passacaille, Op. 25
2121-02 and string bass
MP (Paris: Lemoine)

Chabrier, Emmanuel (French, 1841–1894), arr. Grovlez

Danse Villageoise & *Trois Piéces Pittoresques*
1122-02
MS [perhaps an arrangement for Taffanel]

Cossart, Leland (French, b. 1877)

Suite, Op. 19
2222-02, Eng. hn and harp
MP (Magdeburg: Heinrichshofen, 1908)
    This set has the original Longy Club stamp.

Dubois, Theodore (French, 1837–1924)

Première Suite
2122-01
MP (Paris: Heugel, 1898)

Deuxième Suite, for 2122-01
MP (Paris: Leduc)

Flament, Edouard (French, 1880–1958)

Fantasia con Fuga, Op. 28
1112-01, Eng. hn
    This set has the original Longy Club stamp.

Franck, César (French, 1822–1890), arr. Humphrey

Pastorale, Op. 19
1122-01, Eng. horn
MS [MS]

Gounod, Charles

Petite Symphonie
1222-02
MP (Paris: Costallat, 1904)

Holbrooke, Joseph (English, 1878-1958, known as 'the cockney Wagner')

Sextett, Nr. 3, Op. 33
MP (London: Chester, 1922)

Huré, Jean (French, 1877–1930)

Pastorale
3222-02
MS (Duclos Copying House)
    This set has the original Longy Club stamp.

d'Indy, Vincent

Chansons et Danses, Op. 50
2122-01
MP (Paris: Durand)

Sarabande et Menuet
MP (Paris: Hamelle)

Lachner, Franz

Octett, Op. 156
1122-02
MP (early print, publisher not given)

Leleu, Jeanne (French, b. 1898)

Suite Symphonique
2111-21, Eng. horn, piano and percussion
MP (Paris: Leduc, 1926)

Monteux, Pierre (French, 1875–1964)

Deux Piécettes
1111-1, percussion
MP (Paris: Zunz Mathot)

Moreau, Léon (French, 1784–1841)

Nocturne
2222-02
MS

Mouqet, Jules (French, b. 1860)

Suite, for 1122-01
MP (Paris: Lemoine, 1910)

Symphoniette, Op. 12
2222-02
MS
     This set has the original Longy Club stamp.

Onslow, George (Anglo-French, 1784–1853)

Septuor, Op. 79
MP (Paris: Hamelle)

Pascal, ? (French, nineteenth century)

Octuor
1112-11, piccolo
MP (Paris: Durand, 1947)

Pierné, Gabriel (French, 1863–1937)

Preludio et Fughetta
2112-02
MP (Paris: Hamelle)

Reinecke, Carl (German, 1824–1910)

Octett
1122-02
MP (Leipzig: Breitkopf & Härtel)

Rheinberger, Josef (German, 1839–1901)

Sextett, Op. 191b
MP (Leipzig: Leuckart)

Saint-Saëns, arr. Taffanel

Feuillet d'Album
1122-02
MP (Paris: Durand)

Wagner, Eugéne (nineteenth century composer)

Suite
2222-, piano
MS
    This set has the original Longy Club stamp.

THE ST. LOUIS WIND ENSEMBLE REPERTOIRE

The St. Louis Wind Ensemble consisted of members of the St. Louis Symphony Orchestra, the oldest orchestra in America, and was formed by the English hornist of that orchestra, Alfred H. Hicks (1898–1976). The basic instrumentation of the ensemble was a double wind quintet and the surviving library is owned by his daughter, Barbara Hicks Garton of Columbus, IN. Michael Finkelmann examined this collection and reports the following ensemble works.

Hicks, Alfred (1898–1976)

Improvisation & Allegro (1961)
solo oboe and small band

Sir Nigel

Theme and Variations

Tournament Overture (1936)
 Performed in 1978 at a memorial concert at Eastern Illinois University

Tower of Babel

Beethoven, arr. Hicks

'Allegro' from *Symphony Nr. 8* (1941)
10 winds

Debussy, arr. Hicks

First Arabesque
10 winds

Second Arabesque
2222, piccolo, Eng. hn, bass clarinet, contrabsn

Godard, Benjamin (French, 1849–1895), arr. Hicks

Scènes Poétiques
10 winds

Goossens, arr. Hicks

Hommage à Debussy (1931)

Lalo, Édouard (French, 1823–1892), arr. Hicks

Symphonie espagnole
violin and wind ensemble

MacDowell, Edward (American, 1860–1908), arr. Hicks

Woodland Sketches
wind ensemble

Mendelssohn, arr. Hicks

Rondo Capriccioso (1941)
double wind quintet

Schubert, arr. Hicks

L'Abeille, Op. 13
violin solo and 1122-

THE BAND ARRANGEMENTS BY LEOPOLD STOKOWSKI

On the afternoon of May 18, 1924, before a full house in the famous Academy of Music in Philadelphia, the school boy tuba player—turned famous organist—turned renowned conductor, Leopold Stokowski, conducted a full-length band concert. But this was not just any band concert, this was a concert by a band he himself had created and he called it the Philadelphia Band. When the curtain went up the audience saw 120 musicians in gold uniforms and a local newspaper reported, according to Mencken,

> There were cheers, shouts and stamping of feet by an audience that refused to be silenced. The concert was a sensational triumph even before a note had been played.

While we know Stokowski was a man of very broad interests, I do not believe there is much known about how he got the idea to create this band. It almost has to have been a musical idea. Having been a professional church organist earlier in his career, I believe it was likely that he had in mind creating a 'live organ,' so to speak. The entire history of the organ lay in its being a surrogate wind band, beginning at a time when the live makers of wind sound were not admitted in the church building (before the seventeenth century). Even today, if you do not use the slurpy, sweet vibrato of the string stops, what you hear in an organ is a great wind band sound, with many of the actual stops still named after wind instruments.

In any case the idea to create this band must have occurred long before this concert because Stokowski set to work preparing, in his own hand, a number of large-scale transcriptions for wind band. From this concert alone we know he made transcriptions of the:

Strauss, *Blue Danube Waltz*
Sibelius, *Finlandia*
Schubert's '*Moment Musical*'
Wagner's 'Entrance of the gods into Valhalla' from *Das Rheingold*
      Wotan's Farewell and the *Feuerzauber* from *Die Walküre*
      The funeral march from *Götterdämmerung*
Bach, *Passacaglia*

Following the well-known tradition of Sousa, Stokowski surrounded the above compositions with encores consisting of Sousa marches. However, as any musician who knew the concerts of Stokowski would understand, the goal of the performance of the marches remained one of very high musicianship. One of America's most famous literary critics of the day, H. L. Mencken, in *On Music* (New York: Knopf, 1961), 121, attended this concert and on this subject he added a very interesting paragraph.

> Even the Sousa marches showed some new touches. Sousa himself used to play them with the aid of double-basses and a huge battery of percussion instruments. Stokowski omitted the double-basses and reduced the percussion to its usual orchestral strength, with only one bass drum and one set of timpani. The effect was

superb. All the familiar rattle was gone; instead there was a clear, bell-like lively sonority—a magnificent swirl of pure sound. If Sousa was not in the house he missed something. His marches were played perfectly for the first time.

One is rather surprised to find the sophisticated Mencken in the audience, but he had in fact made a trip from Baltimore in order to hear this concert and his comments on the concert make it clear it was a true concert and not an entertainment event.

Bands, of course, are numerous, and many of them are good ones. But this is a band of an entirely new sort. Stokowski has neither tried to batter his audience into unconsciousness with mere noise, in the manner of the Italian conductors, nor endeavored to make his band an imitation orchestra, in the fashion of John Philip Sousa. Instead he has sought, within the natural limits of his medium, to augment its flexibility, its variety, its dignity—in brief, to convert it only a first-rate musical instrument …

The concert really began with the *Einzug* from *Das Rheingold*. Here Stokowski achieved double triumph: first with his scoring and then with his conducting. The familiar music leaped into new life at the first note: one presently began lamenting that Wagner had written it for orchestra, not for band. There was endless variety and endless charm in the tone color. Exquisite combinations followed one another enchantingly …

But in the *Feuerzauber* Stokowski offered some effects of the very first caliber—not imitation orchestra effects, but undisguised band effects, yet how delicate always, how charmingly appropriate to the music! The *pianissimo* of the band toward the end became almost fairylike. It seemed incredible that the great gang of men could play with so soft and exquisite a touch. The audience sat as silent as the dead.

The band gave another concert or two and then disappeared forever. Perhaps Stokowski simply did not have enough quality music available to him to maintain his interest.

We know of a few more transcriptions by Stokowski, the 'Air on the G string' from the *Suite in D*, a Bach chorale, *'Wir glauben all' an einen Gott'* as well has some marches in his hand, the Sousa *El Capitan* and the J. F. Wagner *Under the Double Eagle*.

The U.S. Marine Band library in Washington, D.C., has an undisclosed number of the Stokowski transcriptions, but where are the rest?

THE WHITWELL ARCHIV COLLECTION, TROSSINGEN, GERMANY

In 2000, as preparation for my retirement in 2005, I began the process of shipping my library to the *Bundesakademie für musikalische Jugendbildung*, in Trossingen, Germany, the most important graduate music education institution in Europe. Their initial request for my collection, together with their modern library facilities, first-rate staff, technical facilities and promise to create a separate 'Whitwell Archiv' was an offer I could not refuse. Among the materials I gave them were the following.

- Some 2,000 score and parts for early wind band music. The *Bundesakademie* has now catalogued most of this collection and has published a beautiful index of this music, *Archiv David Whitwell: Verzeichnis der Noten*, in both soft cover form and in CD form which they sell for a very modest price. There are many additional works one can see, if visiting the *Bundesakademie Bibliothek*, which they elected not to catalog, such as the complete works for winds by Liszt, Bruckner, and other nineteenth-century prints together with many early anonymous works.

- Several hundred books, many with author's signatures, some very rare and some previously owned by important persons, such as an original print of the *Creation* (1800), in a copy which belonged to Haydn himself.

- Some 50 boxes of my original correspondence, 1964–2000, including autograph letters from many famous composers and musicians.

- A large collection of eighteenth-century engravings and other rare iconography, together with an eighteenth-century French hunting horn.

- A complete collection of my articles and books through 2000, as well as extensive collections of various journals.

- A collection of rare early band recordings, including Liberati, Creature, Conway, *Garde Republicaine* of Paris, Arthur Pryor, *Banda Citta di Rome*, Minichini, Victor Herbert, the Longy Club, the Curtis Wind Ensemble and various soloists of Sousa. Curiosities include a 1926 recording of Ormandy as a violinist and one of the only recordings of a castrato who lived into the age of recordings.

- A large tape collection of live performances by the California State University, Northridge Wind Ensemble, David Whitwell, conducting. These tapes are live recordings of professional level performance quality which I assembled for the use by European conducting students who attend the frequent conducting clinics hosted by the *Bundesakademie* for the repertoire, of course, carries my personal recommendation.

For the reader's information, this collection of recorded performances include the following compositions:

Aleppo, Giancarlo. *Prima Lux*
_____, *Cogitationes*
Van Ammelsvoort, Jos. *French Overture*
Bach, J. S. *Capriccio on the Departure of his Brother*
_____, *Toccata & Fugue in D minor*
Badings, Henk. *Armageddon*
_____, *Sinfonietta Nr. II*
Batiste, Edouard (19th c.) *Sinfonie*
Beglarian, Grant. *Sinfonia*
Beethoven. *Siegessinfonie*
Benson, Warren. *Dawn's Early Light*
Berlioz. *Symphony for Band*
_____, *Overture to Beatrice and Benedict*
Brahms. *Begräbnisgesang* for band and chorus
Broege, Timothy. *Sinfonia XVI, Transcendental Vienna*
Carafa, Michele (19th c.). *Allegretto* for solo clarinet and winds
_____, *Andante* for solo horn and winds
Casella, Alfredo. *Introduzione Corale e Marcia*, conducted by Ronald Johnson
Clarke, Nigel. *Samurai*
Connor, Bill. *Tails of the Vienna Woods*
Copland, Aaron. *Emblems*
Cushing, Charles. *Angel Camp*
Ellerby, Martin. *Venetian Spells*
Erickson, Frank. *Time and the Winds*
Fasch, Johann (Baroque). *Concerto for Three Bands*
Fauchet, Paul. *Symphony in Bb*
Fletcher, Grant. *Concerto for Winds*
Flippa, Giuseppe (19th c.). *Marcia funebre*
Francaix, Jean. *Sept danses apres 'Les malheurs de Sophie'*
Franck, Cesar. *Choral Nr. 2*
Gallo, Vincenzo (19th c.). *Piccola Sinfonia*
Gorb, Adam. *Yiddish Dances*
Gossec, Francois (18th c.). *Hymn to Liberty*
_____, *Le Triomphe de la Loi*
_____, *Marche lugubre*
_____, *Te Deum*
Gotkovsky, Ida. *Symphonie pour Orchestre d'Harmonie*
_____, *Poem du Feu*

Gould, Morton. *Concertette for Viola and Band*

Grainger, Percy. *Lincolnshire Posy*

_____, *Marching Song for Democracy*

_____, *Gum Suckers March*

_____, *Irish Tune*

Gulda, Friedrich. *Concerto for Cello and Wind Orchestra*

Halevy, Jacques (19th c.) *Marche Heroique*

Hidas, Frigyes, *Save the Sea Symphony*

_____, *Coriolanus*

Hindemith. *Symphony for Band*

Holst, Gustav. *Suite in F*, Karel Husa conducting

_____, *Music for a London Pageant*

_____, *Hammersmith*

Hovhaness, Alan. *Symphony Nr. 4*

Hummel, Johann (19th c.) *Trumpet Concerto* (Tony Plog)

Husa, Karel. *Apotheosis of this Earth*

_____, *Concerto for Wind Ensemble*

_____, *Concerto for Trumpet*

_____, *Concerto for Saxophone*

_____, *Les Couleurs Fauves*

_____, *Music for Prague, 1968*

Hutcheson, Jere. *Caricatures*

Ito, Yasuhide. *Glorioso*

Jadin, Hyacinthe (18th c.). *Ouverture*

von Karajan, Herbert. *The European Anthem*

Kling, Henri (19th c.). *Hommage a Haydn*

Loechlin, Charles. *Chant de Louis XIII*

Lancen, Serge. *Aunis et Saintonge en Fête*

_____, *Symphonie de L'Eau*

Larsen, Libby. *Grand Rondo, Napoleon dances the Cancan*

Lefevre, Xavier (18th c.). *Marche militaire*

Linn, Robert. *Propagula*

Lukas, Zdenek. *Musica Boehma*

Mahler. *Um Mitternacht*

_____, *Symphony Nr. 5*, first movement [arr.]

Mascagni, arr. Carl Ruggles. Introduction and Siciliana from *Cavalleria Rusticana*

Maschek, Paul (19th c.) *The Battle of Leipzig*

_____, *The Occupation of Paris*

_____, *Austria's Triumph*

Maslanka, David. *Symphony Nr. 2*

Maw, Nicholas. American Games

McCoy, David. *A Symphony for Salem, 1692*

Mehul, Etienne (18th c.). *Ouverture*

Mejo, Guillaume (19th c.). *Variations on 'Gaudeamus igitur'*

Mendelssohn, Felix. *Festgesang*

_____, *Overture for Band*

_____, *Fingal's Cave Overture*, Felix Hauswirth conducting

Mertens, Hardy. *U Mundu Drentu A Ti*

Messiaen. *Et Exspecto Resurrectionem Mortuorum*

Meyerbeer. *Torch Dance Nr. 2*

Miaskovsky, Nikolai. *Symphony Nr. 19*

Milhaud, Darius. *Suite Française*

Mozart. *Partita in C minor*, K.384a

Munchs, C. (19th c.) *Overture a Grande Harmonie*

Naylor, Craig. *Convivial Tides*

Nielsen, Carl. *Paraphrase on 'Nearer My God to Thee'*

Ochs, Siegfried. *Variations on 'Kommt a Vogel geflogen'*

Orrego-Salas, Juan. *Concerto for Wind Orchestra*

Penderecki, Krzysztof. *Pittsburgh Overture*

Pierne, Gabriel (19th c.) *Marche Solennelle*

Ponchielli, Amilcare(19th c.) *Elegia on the Death of Garibaldi*

_____, *Sinfonia in F minor*

_____, *Sinfonia in Bb minor*

_____, *Variations on Carnevale di Venezia*

_____, *Trumpet Concerto*

Poole, Geoff. *Sailing with Archangels*

Reicha, Anton (19th c.) *Commemoration Symphony*

Respighi, Ottorino. *Feste Romane* [arr. Schafer]

Rimsky-Korsakov. *Variations on a Theme of Glinka*

Saint-Saens. *Orient et Occident*

Sallinen, Aulis. *Chorali*

Schmidt-Wunstorf, Rudolf. *Symphony Ardennaise*

Schmitt, Florent. *Marche in Eb*

_____, *Dionysiaques*

Schönberg. *Theme and Variations*

Schubert. *Hymne*, Op. 154

Schumann, Robert. *Beim Abschied zu Singen*, for band and chorus

Schumann, William. *Chester*

Sibelius. *Suite for Band*

Sorcsek, Jerome. *Variations for Band*

_____, *Symphony Nr. 1*

_____, *Symphony Nr. 2*

_____, *Two Chorale Preludes*

Sousa. *Stars & Stripes Forever*

Stokes, Eric. *The 'Continental Harp and Band Report*

Strauss, Richard. *Ein Heldenleben* [arr. Hindsley]

_____, *Rosenkavalier Waltzes* [arr.]

_____, *Suite in Bb*, Op. 4

_____, *Feierlicher Einzug*

_____, *Also Sprach Zarathustra* [arr. Hindsley]

_____, *Till Eulenspiegel* [arr. Hindsley]

_____, *Don Juan* [arr Hindsley.]

Stravinsky, Igor. *Le Sacre du Printemps* [arr. Whitwell]

Surinach, Carlos. *Paens and Dances of Heathern Iberia*

Tchaikowsky. *Romeo and Juliet Fantasy* [arr. Hindsley]

_____, *Capriccio Italian* [arr. Hindsley]

Verdi. Excerpts from the *Manzoni Requiem* [arr. Whitwell]

_____, *Overture, La Forza del Destino*

Villa-Lobos, *Fantasy in the form of a Choros*, Ronald Johnson conducting

Vitaliti, Sebastiano (19th c.) *Sinfonia, La Corona d'Italia*

Von Weber. *Concertino for Oboe*

Wagner. *Rienzi Overture*

_____, *Excerpts from the Ring* [arr. Whitwell]

Whitwell. Symphony Nr. 1, *The Viennese Legacy*

_____, Symphony Nr. 2, *Sinfonia da Requiem*

_____, Symphony Nr. 3, *Meditations on Hamlet*

_____, Symphony Nr. 4, *Symphony of Songs*

_____, Symphony Nr. 5, *Sinfonia Italia*

Widmer, Ernst. *Variations on 'l'homme arme*

Many of the scores and parts for the early works can be obtained from www.whitwellbooks.com.

Suggestions for Future Research

WITH THIS VOLUME I bring to a close fifty-five years of enjoyment in exploring long forgotten wind band repertoire as an avocation, a hobby really, contiguous to my very active career as a conductor. The story of how this research began reflects a peculiar aspect of music education in the United States, a characteristic not found in Europe, and that is the fact that the world of music education here is not really part of the world of professional music. There are a number of men here whom, if you refer to them as band conductors, will correct you by saying, 'I am not a *conductor*, I am a band *director*.' My perspective on music-making being what it is, I have never understood what is meant by this distinction.

While a student at the University of Michigan I was fortunate to live in an old rooming-house on campus which was populated by horn players, among them H. Robert Reynolds, Howard Howard (later Principal horn in the Metropolitan Opera) and Karl Glenn. This old house was adjacent to a bell tower which at that time housed the library of the School of Music. Being an aspiring young conductor it became my habit to go next door, as time allowed, obtain a score and a recording and return to my room to practice conducting great orchestral compositions. One day, for some reason, I decided to study and conduct one of the major works by Richard Strauss. Upon reaching the appropriate place on a library shelf I was disappointed to find the score I wanted missing. But next to the empty space was a score which read, on the cover, *Symphony for Winds*, by Richard Strauss! I was astounded to find such a score, which was so much more important musically than the repertoire being performed by the university band in which I was a member. I checked this score out and took it to Dr. William D. Revelli to inquire more about this work. Considering the fact that Strauss was one of the most famous composers living during his own lifetime, I was quite bewildered to discover that Revelli knew nothing about this score and, indeed, had never heard of it. The immediate implication for me was, of course, that the library may be filled with such scores which lay outside the knowledge of most band conductors. And so it was, and so began my avocation.

Apart from the thrill of the hunt, a particular reward in looking for early wind repertoire over the years has been the consequent making of many friends among professional musicians in Europe. One of these musicians, Jimmy Brown, second oboist for many years with the English Chamber Orchestra, and I used to cross paths many times in European libraries. I used to leave him, in obscure volumes of oboe music I knew he would run across some day, little slips of paper welcoming him. And he once found, in a very small library in Madrid, a rare copy of published military band music by Franz Krommer which he knew I would be interested in. In this uncataloged library the music was simply lying in cardboard boxes marked 'piano' or 'oboe,' etc., and it was in the latter that he found the Krommer early publication. He knew immediately I would be interested—but what to do with it? He reasoned that if he gave it to the librarian as something misplaced in the 'oboe box' there would be no predicting where the librarian would deposit it. Leaving it in the 'oboe box' might result in the same fate when found by some later person. So, Jimmy hid it and drew a map where I could find it in this room. I kept that map for more than twenty years before I had occasion to go to Madrid to rest from jet-lag before doing a big concert in Lisbon. But when that moment came, I could not find the map! It had become misplaced during the move from Los Angeles to Texas. Now I have found it again and it waits for another trip to Madrid.

Well, as that interesting score waits to be found so there are, of course, many more early scores waiting to be found by some future person working in this field. Following are some of the subjects given me by friends in Europe which I have maintained in a folder of future research projects and which I can now foresee I shall never have the time to study. I recommend them all and hope that their very scope will reflect how much more needs to be done.

A LOST WORK BY GUSTAV HOLST

Near the end of his life, Holst was asked by Associated Sound Film Industries at Wembley, England, to compose some music for a film called 'The Bells' based on an adaptation of J. R. Ware's *The Polish Jew*. Early in the work Holst became very enthusiastic, writing to Adeline Vaughn Williams, 'I have written quite of lot of music that makes me purr and feel good all over.'

What happened next is reviewed by Michael Short in his biography of Holst [*Gustav Holst*, Oxford University Press, 1990, 298].

> For some reason the company made little effort to distribute the film. Although its imminent release was announced in the press in 1931 and again in 1932, this produced few advance bookings and it was eventually sold off to an American company. It seems that the film was never shown in the USA either, and neither the American company nor the present whereabouts of the film can now be traced. Holst's score and parts have apparently disappeared just as completely, and the only person who could recall the music was an official of Associated Sound Films, who remembered a two-track sequence in which a brass band and a pipe band, playing their own tunes, marched from different directions and came together …

For some years I made an attempt through a musicologist who worked for one of the large film industries in Los Angeles to find this film but no trace of it could be found. I hope others will continue to look for the original music of this film as it may contain some valuable music for band.

A LOST WORK BY MAHLER

Alma Mahler, in her biographical work on her husband, makes reference to a private festival, held at the University of Vienna in May, 1902, in honor of Max Klinger, who had made a monument of Beethoven. Mahler was asked to conduct the music for the opening of the festival. He not only agreed, but made for the occasion a transcription for winds and chorus of a portion of the *Ninth Symphony* of Beethoven. As Alma Mahler, his widow, relates,

> He arranged part of the chorus from the Ninth Symphony for wind and brass instruments only, and rehearsed it with the wind and brass members of the Opera orchestra [the Vienna Philharmonic].
>
> *Ihr stürzt nieder, Millionen?*
> *Ahnest Du den Schöpfe, Welt?*
> *Such' ihn über'm Sternenzelt.*
> *Über Stenen muss er wohnen.*
>
> Mahler conducted the chorus on the day and with the new instrumentation it rang out as starkly as granite. Klinger, who was a very shy man, came in just as the first note sounded out above his head. He was so moved that tears ran slowly down his cheeks.

Where is this score? When I lived in Vienna, in 1968–1969, I looked for it in all the major libraries, including the Philharmonic library and the private library of Mahler's publisher, Universal Edition. A friend at Universal Edition did bring out a score they said at that time was unknown, a published score of Beethoven's *Ninth Symphony* which Mahler used to add in very small red ink a greatly expanded wind section. Maybe that is what was used on the occasion described above, although I doubt it for as I recall his work in this case included the entire symphony. But, no one had heard of a separate wind arrangement of Beethoven's *Ninth*. I fear it was lost when Alma's apartment was bombed during the war.

THE TANGLEWOOD WIND ENSEMBLE

The correspondent we have introduced earlier, Michael Finkelman, has also written of a period early in the twentieth century when there was a Wind Ensemble at Tanglewood. If it indeed began in the 1930s then we may presume that, like the Curtis Institute Wind Ensemble, it was inspired by the Longy Club, the wind ensemble consisting of members of the Boston Symphony. Given the association between the Boston Symphony Orchestra and Tanglewood, it would be no surprise to find that Longy himself played some role in the founding of this wind ensemble.

> Speaking of wind ensembles conducted by oboists, there was the one formed in the early 1930s at Tanglewood by Louis Speyer, who was also quite a conductor. This was also an all-student group of around 12–20 players, which he directed every summer for more than 40 years. As a result, there are some rarities in the library there, including the Caplet.

A study of the history of this wind ensemble and a search in the Tanglewood library for its repertoire would be a valuable project.

THE NEW YORK SYMPHONY QUINTET

This ensemble was founded by George Barrère (1876–1944), who had been a student of Paul Taffanel at the Paris Conservatory. In 1895, the year he graduated from the conservatory with a first prize, he founded, in Paris, the *La Société Moderne d'Instruments à Vent*, which continued the tradition of the older *La Société de Musique de Chambre pour instruments à vent* which had been organized by his teacher, Taffanel. The reader will recall that it was for Taffanel's society that Gounod composed his *Symphony* for winds.

This new ensemble was responsible for commissioning, among other works, the Roussel *Divertissement*, Op. 6, for piano and winds (1914) and the Schmitt *Lied et Scherzo*, Op. 54 (1910), for ten winds. A publication in the American magazine, *The Metronome*, in 1911 made an interesting observation about this ensemble.

> This society has proved a stimulus to modern composers, enabling them to realize the expressive qualities, peculiar sonority and special effects resulting from the combination of flute, oboe, clarinet, French horn and bassoon employed in single or double quintette with or without piano. During the sixteen years of its existence this society has produced no less than 100 new compositions by 50 different composers and has been subsidized by the Government in recognition of its service to general musical advancement. Colonne, Massenet, Saint-Saens, Widor, d'Indy and Faure are a few of the many prominent musicians bearing testimony to the unique achievements of this organization.

As this account implies, this ensemble existed until 1911 but its founder, George Barrère, left Paris in 1905 to assume the position of principal flute with the New York Symphony. The New York papers of this period praised Barrère for his beauty of tone and brilliant execution.

Soon after his arrival in New York, Barrère organized the *New York Symphony Quintet*. The other members of the quintet were,

Cesare Addimando, oboe
Léon Leroy, a clarinetist who had studied with Rose in Paris and was a soloist with the *Garde Republicaine* band before coming to New York.
Hermann Hand, horn, a native and student in Vienna, where he had been a member of both the court opera and the civic opera.
Auguste Mesnard, bassoon, a native of Cognac, France, but a student of the Paris Conservatory where he won first prize in theory and bassoon. Before coming to New York he was a soloist in the *Concerts-Lamoureux* and in the Paris Opera.

The establishment of this ensemble was noticed in Paris by one of its most famous composers.

Dear Mr. George Barrère:
    In continuing in New York the work of the *La Société Moderne d'Instruments à Vent*, which you so successfully founded in Paris, you will contribute to the development of Musical Art in America by introducing to the American public many highly interesting works too little known in that country.
    My best wishes are with you. I have no doubt your enterprise will be crowned with success.
    Most devotedly,

Camille Saint-Saëns

The Metronome, published in New York, in its issue of April, 1907, contains an article on this ensemble, as well as a photograph. Here we read,

> That musical culture and taste is greatly on the increase and that there is a decided demand for the artistic in musical performances can be demonstrated in no stronger way than by calling attention to and discussing the objects of such an organization as 'The New York Symphony Quintet.'
>
> What more delightful combination can be imagined than the associating of a Flute, an Oboe, a Clarinet and a Bassoon, strengthened and ennobled by the peculiar tonal qualities of a French Horn?
>
> When considering the natural beauties and possibilities of five such instruments placed in the hands of exceptional artists, nothing but artistic and gratifying results may be expected. This quintet is composed of five soloists of the New York Symphony Orchestra, which, under the leadership of Mr. Walter Damrosch, is considered as one of the best symphony concert organizations of this or any other country …
>
> To return once more to the Symphony Quintet, we must mention its very extensive repertoire, including compositions by the classic writers such as Bach, Mozart, Beethoven, Schubert and Mendelssohn, and Saint-Saëns, Ruinstein, Gounod, Pierne, Reinecke, Dubois, Dvorak, Vincent d'Indy and E. Pessard among the moderns.

The reader will notice that the repertoire mentioned here is not, strictly speaking, quintet repertoire. Indeed, it resembles more the larger repertoire of the Longy Club in Boston and the earlier Taffanel wind ensemble repertoire in Paris.

THE BARRÈRE ENSEMBLE

By 1911 Barrere decided to enlarge his New York ensemble and he now was joined by the following musicians:

Flutes – Barrere and Rocco Guerriere
Horns – Josef Franzel, H. Heyer
Oboes – Albert de Bussacher and Irving Cohn
Bassoons – Benjamin Kohon and Emile Barbot
Clarinets – Henry Leon Leroy and Harry Christman
Trumpet – Carl Heinrich.

The first concert by this ensemble was performed on Monday afternoon, 28 February 1911, at the Stuyvesant Theatre in New York City. The program, assisted by Arthur Whiting on harpsichord, was,

Haydn	Octet in F
Handel	Sonata in B minor for harpsichord and flute
Mozart	Serenade in C minor
Bach	Sonata in E♭ for harpsichord and flute
Beethoven	Octet, Op. 103

The second concert, on 7 March, was much more extended.

Part I – German Composers

Reinecke	Octet, Op. 216
Thuille	Sextette, Op. 5

Part II – French Composers

Pierné	Pastorale Variée dans le style ancient, Op. 30
d'Indy	Chanson et Danses, Op. 50
Hahn	Cimetiere de Campagne
Caplet	Suite Persane

Shortly after these first two concerts, *The Metronome* (New York, April, 1910) devoted an article to this ensemble which contains much interesting information.

It seems a most encouraging sign for the gradual betterment of musical taste to notice the growing interest in music for wood-wind instruments. New York, with its wealth of operatic, symphonic, and string music, has paid comparatively little attention to the unusually interesting literature for wood-wind instruments. This field has not, however, been ignored as much as might be supposed, for we find the greatest composers to have written some of their most beautiful works for just such combinations.

Among writers who have written in this way may be mentioned Bach, Haydn, Handel, Mozart, Beethoven and Spohr, to the later utterances of Schubert, Brahms, Reinecke, Richard Strauss, Gabriel Pierné, Vincent d'Indy and Charles M. Loeffler. While masters of every school have expressed themselves in this interesting form, the difficulty in assembling competent players for continued practice has made the performance of works for wind instruments very rare.

Mr. George Barrère, one of the most accomplished flute players in this country, has started this season to give a number of concerts devoted entirely to the performance of ensemble music for wood-wind instruments and the success which attended his first concert gives promise of a most encouraging future.

His ideas of starting such concerts in New York has been prompted by the fact that in 1895 he founded similar movements in Paris, under the name of *La Société Moderne d'Instruments à vent*, now in its sixteenth year. This society has proved a stimulus to modern composers, enabling them to realize the expressive qualities, peculiar sonority and special efforts resulting from the combination of flute, oboe, clarinet, French horn and bassoon employed in single or double quintette with or without piano. During the sixteen years of its existence this society has produced no less than 100 new works by 50 different composers and has been subsidized by the Government in recognition of its service to general musical advancement. Colonne, Massenet, Saint-Saëns, Widor, d'Indy and Fauré are a few of the many prominent musicians bearing testimony to the unique achievements of this organization.

I personally do not know how long this ensemble continued to exist in New York, but surely the local newspapers must have much more information about the ensemble in subsequent years. Clearly it is a topic most worthy of further research.

It appears that no recordings were made of this ensemble, however Barrère himself did make a number of recordings of his own playing beginning in 1914. My good friend, Frederick P. Williams, told me he had all of the recordings made by Barrère in his remarkable collection of early recordings [now at UC Santa Barbara].

THE TAFFANEL WOODWIND ENSEMBLE

In my book on the Longy Club wind ensemble of Boston (www.whitwellbooks.com) I have given considerable information on the famous ensemble founded by Paul Taffanel, the *La Société de Musique de Chambre pour instruments à vent*, including a list of their repertoire. Taffanel discontinued his participation in this ensemble by 1895 when he became a full-time opera conductor. Georges Longy and George Barrère were both involved in the later history of this ensemble in Paris before they each moved to New York.

There seems to have continued some kind of wind ensemble activity in Paris for in the 1930s recordings were made of an ensemble called the *Taffanel Woodwind Ensemble*. My friend Williams owned several of these issued on the RCA Victor label, Album M-137 (7578, 7579 and 7580). The repertoire on these recording included the Mozart *Quintet* for piano and winds and the Thuille *Gavotte*.

Once again, here is an ensemble most worthy of further study.

THE BRUSSELS SOCIÉTÉ D'INSTRUMENTS À VENT

The reader has seen how the original French wind ensemble activity under Taffanel was widespread in its influence. No doubt there were many subsequent ensembles which also deserve further study. One of these existed in Brussels during the late nineteenth century and I have heard the speculation that the famous oboist Guillaume Guidé was the leader of this ensemble.

THE FRANSELLA WIND ENSEMBLE IN LONDON

A potentially very interesting man was Albert Francella (ca. 1866–1934), who was known as the 'Paganini of the flute.' Born in Holland, he was encouraged by Brahms, who assured him of a brilliant career. After a time Fransella moved to London where he performed with the major orchestras, became a professor at the Guildhall School of Music and at Trinity College and formed a trio with Léon Goossens and Francesco Ticciati.

For years correspondents have mentioned to me concerts by a larger wind ensemble under Fransella. Such an ensemble would have included the best players in London and one would assume its activities were extensively covered in the London press.

THE LONDON CIVIL BAND OF 1912

The *London Musical Times* for 1 November 1912, contains a brief review of a concert by this newly formed band, conducted by one Emile Gilmer. The *Times* called this the 'most interesting feature of the present season' and mentions that composers had been asked to compose for it. Most interesting of all is the claim by the *Times* that the whole idea of this band was the inspiration of the famous Sir Thomas Beecham, who wanted to 'arrest the alleged decline of English wind playing and to explore new sources of tone-coulour.'

Fortunately, the *Times* also mentioned the instrumentation of this new 'London Civil Band,' which it listed as follows:

2 piccolos
2 flutes
2 oboes
bass oboe
heckelphone
English horn
2 E♭ clarinets
8 B♭ clarinets
2 basset horns
2 bass clarinets
2 bassoons
sarrusophone in B♭
sarrusophone in C
soprano saxophone
alto saxophone
tenor saxophone
baritone saxophone
2 trumpets
cornet à pistons in E♭
bass trumpet
4 horns
3 trombones (alto, tenor, bass)
3 tubas, in F, E♭ and B♭
celesta
timpani
side drum
bass drum and cymbals
harp

ON LIBRARIES

Since this chapter is addressed to the subject of future research I cannot fail to say a word about libraries. I have been in more than one library in Europe which had cataloged its 'aesthetic' music with great care, but had to lead me to a closed room where the military band music existed, uncataloged, in card-board boxes. In spite of the recent efforts of R.I.S.M. to catalog manuscripts in Europe, it will be a very long time before they get to military bands.

One must be honest and admit there is a residual prejudice involved here, although it is not so strong as it once was—as in the era when all wind music was called 'Tafel musik' and where the string players were classified as artists the wind players were classified as household servants. This prejudice I once encountered in a very important library where I noticed a number of cards in the file contained a red 'X' at the top of the card. It was explained to me that this symbol represented those works which would be hastily removed if there were the fear of the building being bombed during WWII. No wind scores had a red 'X.'

I can assure the reader there is much more to do in libraries and many exciting discoveries yet to be made. Think of St. Petersburg, where surely are housed the band compositions by Rimsky-Korsakov, not to mention the library of the Kaiser, Alexander III (1885–1894) who maintained a band in which all the players were members of the aristocracy and which gave private concerts. And where are the scores Strauss conducted during his several visits to Spain when he guest conducted his major tone poems with band?

There are two projects in the United States which we should not overlook. One collection is the New York City Public Library. A correspondent wrote me in 1990,

> There are fully 8,000 manuscripts by American composers in the process of being cataloged (at the flow rate of cold molasses) in the New York Public Library. I have no doubt that there are a goodly few wind ensemble items in this copious collection.

Another very interesting subject for study is.quite curious, a large collection of documents belonging to the Paris Conservatory of Music which has found its way to the Boston University Library. A letter by Margaret Goostray, Assistant Director of Special Collections, dated 19 July 1988, suggests how valuable this collection is.

> You ask about the Paris Conservatoire de Musique records which we have. These are original papers, not photocopies or films of materials elsewhere. The papers date largely from the middle third of the 19th century and consist of correspondence, official reports, rules and regulations of the institution, records of programs and performances by famous artists, material of directors of the institution (Cherubini, Auber, Thomas, Fauré, and others) and files of Liszt, Gounod, Massenet, Saint-Saëns, Halévy, Debussy.

During my very brief conversations with the staff there seemed to be no knowledge regarding how this material ended up in Boston. But with the nineteenth-century movement of so many wind players from Paris to Boston, not to mention the fact that the Paris Conservatory of Music had begun as a band school, do stimulate our curiousity.

ON OUR PREDECESSORS

The history of the wind band is finally coming into view, with respect to its institutions and its repertoire. However, a great deal of work remains with respect to its people. It is impossible to completely separate a man from his music, as is obvious with persons like Mozart and Beethoven. Knowing more about some of the earlier band conductors would surely stimulate our interest in their music. As a personal example, I have known of Karl Komzak's (1850–1905) *The Girls of Baden Waltz* for fifty years, but my first real interest in him came when I read that he slipped and fell under a train while, being late, running to conduct a band rehearsal. Can we identify with that? This man is virtually forgotten, yet in Vienna he sleeps but a few feet from Beethoven.

And what, really, do any of us know about Ponchielli, a working band director and composer of more than seventy original compositions for band of the highest quality? He happened to write a very popular opera, containing an immortal melody, and so his name is written in the sky but his band music went into the closet.

One person whom I believe is in great need of an English biography which would expand our understanding of his wind music is Anton Reicha. There was a time when the man was famous in Paris. In Balzac's 1838 novel, *Les Employées*, a character named Colleville (principal clarinetist in the Opéra Comique) is walking down the street and, turning to a friend, says,

> You should come to our place to hear a concert next Tuesday. We will play a *quintetto* by Reicha.

Anton Reicha (1770–1836), must have been a very interesting man. While a student at the University of Bonn in 1789 he met and became a lifelong friend of Beethoven. After moving to Paris in 1808 he found little appreciation for his compositions, most probably being too austere for the French taste. He became well established as a professor at the Conservatoire and his students included Liszt, Berlioz, Gounod and Franck.

We find a rare contemporary portrait of Reicha in the 1826 encyclopedia of music by John Sainsbury.

> Reicha is still in the vigor of life, of middle stature, and most urbane manners, his general courtesy greatly endearing him to strangers, to whom he is uniformly obliging. He has often expressed to this writer his wish to write an oratorio for the English in the style of their favorite Handel.
>
> In private life he is cheerful and amiable; his favorite amusement is a game of tric-trac. His rooms are decorated with a profusion of elegant and curious articles, which have been presented to him by numerous individuals in public and private life, as testimonies of friendship and of the respect and admiration due to his genius and perseverance …
>
> Reicha's skill has been shown in a variety of compositions, but especially in some admirable quintets, composed expressly for the flute, clarinet, cor Anglois [sic], French horn and bassoon; these are performed frequently at *L'Ecole des Fils d'Apollon*, and, indeed, on all occasions when first-rate performers on the appropriate instruments assemble together.

No description, no imagination, can do justice to these compositions. The effect produced by the extraordinary combinations of apparently opposite-toned instruments, added to Reicha's vigorous style of writing and judicious scoring, have rendered these quintets the admiration of the musical world.

The rapidly changing tastes in nineteenth-century music found Reicha's music a bit cold and academic. One can see evidence of this in the autobiography of Ludwig Spohr.

Two days ago I heard two more quite new quintets of Reicha, which he wrote for the morning-concerts … They were played at a rehearsal, which appears to me to have been given solely for the purpose of fishing for more subscribers to the morning-concerts, among the numerous persons who were invited … It is sad to see what means artists here are obliged to resort to, in order to procure support for their undertakings. While the Parisians press eagerly forward to every sensual enjoyment, they must be almost dragged to intellectual ones …

I found the composition of these two new quintets, like those I had previously heard at Kreutzer's, rich in interesting sequences of harmony, correct throughout in the management of the voices and full of effect in the use made of the tone and character of the different wind instruments, but on the other hand, frequently defective in the form. Mr. Reicha is not economical enough of his ideas, and at the very commencement of his pieces he frequently gives from four to five themes, each of which concludes in the tonic. Were he less rich, he would be richer. His formal sections also are frequently badly connected and sound as though he had written one yesterday and the other today. Yet the minuets and scherzo, as short pieces, are less open to this objection, and some of them are real masterpieces in form and content. A German soundness of science and capacity are the greatest ornaments of this master.

Berlioz agreed in his own autobiography that he found the famous quintets interesting, but rather cold. Nevertheless he maintained a certain respect from his own study with Reicha at the conservatory. In an eulogy of Reicha which Berlioz published in the Parsian newspaper, *Journal des Débats*, for 3 July 1836, he recalled,

It is to be noted that, despite the apparent severity of Reicha's precepts, none of the living professors has been more prompt than he to recognize an innovation, even if contrary to all admitted rules, if a happy effect resulted from it, and he saw there the germ of progress. In considering how tight the diapers still are in which they would like, in the schools, to keep musical art, one must confess that this merit reveals, in one so gifted, a great honesty of talent and a reasoning ability of the highest order.

One also finds some criticism of his teaching in his later years, some comments about his not paying attention and being distracted in class. But maybe this was only the kind of 'burnout' which all of us experience at some time or other. But we should also remember that he left us one of the most beautiful and important band compositions of our repertoire. In the preface of this composition, written in his own hand, he observed that this score would need a good conductor who would study the score. There is a man we need to know more about.

ON PERFORMANCE PRACTICE IN WIND REPERTOIRE

Finally, just a note to acknowledge that band directors are quite behind the rest of the world of performance when it comes to performance practice. This is an area very much in need of future enlightenment. Mozart is a case in point.

If there were some way we could talk with Mozart about his great masterpiece for winds, his C minor *Partita*, I can imagine someone asking him about those staccato-note cadences in the Minuet, 'Mr. Mozart, just how short should those staccato notes be?' I am quite certain Mozart would answer, in astonishment, 'But those dots have nothing to do with staccato!' Another question we might ask him is what he meant by '*Adagio*'? There is one of his masterpieces which everyone performs at about quarter-note 140 or so, a tempo which does seem 'right,' but which Mozart has called *Adagio*. Clearly this Italian term meant for him something other than speed.

Given only one question to ask him myself, it would be, 'Why didn't you drink that glass of wine you ordered in the little tavern on Ballgasse, behind your apartment in Vienna, on the afternoon of December 2, 1791?' He moved the glass, untouched, over to an acquaintance sitting with him, with a comment to the effect that it was so sad that he had to die so young. To his utterly confused friend, as well as to his family when he returned to his apartment, Mozart appeared perfectly healthy and did not complain of feeling ill. Yet, in a little more than forty-eight hours he was dead. Contemplating on the nature of the thoughts which had taken possession of Mozart's mind, overcoming his interest in his glass of wine, stimulates my thinking about spiritual matters more than anything which happens in organized religion.

But the same could be said of the experience in performing great music. This brings us full circle in the history of wind bands for the ancient Greek philosophers considered us as part of religion, rather than as part of the trade of art. And this is why I have always thought that anyone who managed to make a living in the field of music was very lucky. And is why, when a business man in the next seat on a plane to somewhere asked me what kind of work I did for a living, I responded, 'Sir, I have never had to work for a living!'

Index

Index of Names

A

Abranyi, Emil, b. 1882, Hungarian composer, 123
Addimando, Cesare, oboist in New York ca. 1905, 212
Aeschfachter, Walther, Switzerland composer, b. 1901, 71
Ahl, C., as arranger of Paer's *Griselda*, 51
Alain, Jehan, French, 20th century composer, 72
Albeniz, Enrique, 20th century Spanish composer, arr. Strasser, 190
Albinoni, Tomaso, 1671–1751, Italian composer, 7
Aleppo, Giancarlo, 20th century Italian composer, 202
Alexander III, Russian Kaiser, 1885–1894, 218
Alkan [pseudonym for Charles Morhange], 1813–1888, composer, 193
Altafulla, Ubaldo-Antonio, Italian, 19th century, 55
Amirow, Fikret, b. 1922, Russian composer, 72
Amon, Johann Andreas, 1763–1825, German composer, 10
Amy, Gilbert, b. 1936 in Paris, composer, 72
André, 18th and 19th century publisher in Offenbach, 10, 35, 39, 45, 51, 52, 53
Apostel, Hans Erick, b. 1901, German composer, 72
Atterburg, Kurt Magnus, b. 1887, Swedish composer, 123
Auber, 19th century French composer, 218

B

Bach, J. S., Baroque composer, 89 [fugue scored for band by Holst]; 191 [arranged by Strasser]; 199 [arranged for band by Stokowsky]; 200, 202, 213, 214, 215
Badings, Henk, 20th century German composer, 202
Balzac, 19th century French novelist, 219
Bantock, Sir Granville, 1868–1946, English, composer, 72
Barber, Samuel, b. 1910, American composer, 72
Barbot, Emile, bassoonist in the 1910 Barrère Ensemble in NYC, 214
Baron, 20th century publisher in New York, 139
Barrère, George, 1876–1944, flutist in Paris and New York, 212ff, 216
Barrows, John, b. 1913, American hornist, 73
Bate, Stanley, b. 1913, English, composer, 73
Batiste, Edouard, 19th century French composer, 202
Battiany, Graff Joseph of Hungary, 19th century [dedication] by Druschetzky, 46
Bauer, Marion, b. 1897, American, composer, 73
Baussnera, Waldeman, 1866–1931, composer, 73, 123
Bax, Arnold, 1883–1953, English composer, 123
Beck, Conrad, b. 1901, Swiss, composer, 73, 123
Beckerath, Alfred von, b. 1901, German composer, 73

Bedford, Herbert, 1867–1945, English composer, 124
Beecham, Sir Thomas, 20th century English conductor, 217
Beethoven, 19th century German composer, 45 [unidentified march by unidentified arranger]; 61, 147, 197, 202, 213, 214, 215
Beglarian, Grant, 20th century American composer, 202
Behred, Fritz, b. 1889, Berlin composer, 74
Bellini, Vincenzo, 1801–1835, Italian composer, 55
Benedikt, Walter, 20th century Austrian composer, 74
Benson, Warren, 20th century American composer, 20
Bentzon, Jorgen, b. 1897, Danish composer, 124
Bentzon, Niels, b. 1919, Danish composer, 74, 125
Berezovsky, Nicolay, b. 1900, Russian composer, 74, 125
Berger, Theodor, b. 1905, Austrian composer, 75
Berlioz, Hector, 19th century French composer, 202, 219ff
Bernier, René, b. 1890, Belgium composer, 75
Bialas, Gunter, b. 1907 in Prussian Silesia, composer, 125
Biefeld, Karl, 1866–1944, German composer, 75
Binet, Jean, b. 1893, Swiss composer, 75, 126
Blum, Robert, b. 1900, German composer, 75
Bo & Ma, 20th century publisher in London, 106
Böhme, 20th century publisher in Augsburg, 103, 150, 172
Böhme, J. A., 19th century publisher in Hambourg, 42
Böhmel, Jean August, 18th century publisher in Hambourg, 53
Boieldieu, Adrien, French, 1775–1834, 10 [biographical note]
Boieldieu, jeune , 19th century publisher in Paris, 65
Boisdeffre, René, 1838–1906, French composer, 193
Bonasegla, Carl Philipp, b. 1770, German, 10
Boosey & Hawkes, 20th century publisher in London, 92, 108
Booth, General William, 19th century Salvation Army [dedication], 92
Borck, Edmund von, b. 1906, German composer, 126
Bosse, 20th century publisher in Regensburg, 120
Bote & Bock, 19th century publisher in Berlin, 62, 82, 88
Bowles, Paul, b. 1910, American composer, 75, 126
Brahms. Johannes, 19th century German composer, 202, 215
Brandus, 19th century publisher in Paris, 62
Brawas (Prowo), Pierre, 1697–1757, German composer, 2
Breau, ?, 20th century German composer, 75
Breitkopf & Härtel, 20th century publisher in Leipzig, 40, 112, 123, 184
Bridge, Frank, 1879–1941, English composer, 126
Brizzi & Nicolai, 20th century publisher in Florence, 175
Broege, Timothy, 20th century American composer, 202

H

L

Vaughn Williams, 1872–1958, Ralph, England, 116

Vellones, Pierre, 1889–1939, French composer, 183

Venturini, Francesco, d. 1745, Italian composer, *Variation sur le Menuet par Mademeiselle Venturini a Vienne*, arranged by Druschetzky for Harmoniemusik, 49

Verdi, Giuseppe, 19th century Italian composer, 56 [*Atila*], arranged by Debali]; 205

Verèse, Edgar, b. 1885, Franco-American composer, 116

Verlag der Ges. Rumän Komp., 20th century publisher in Bukarest, 109

Vidal, Paul-Antoine, 1863–1931, French composer, 117

Vierne, Louis, 1870–1937, French composer, 117

Vieweg, 20th century publisher in Berlin, 89

Vignati, Milos, 1897–1966, Czech composer, 183

Viking, 20th century publisher in Kopenhagen, 147

Villa-Lobos, 1887–1959, Heiter, Brazil, 117, 183, 205

Vitaliti, Sebastiano, 19th century Italian composer, 205

Vogel, Johann Christoph, 1756–1788, *Overture de Démophon*, unidentified arranger for Harmoniemusik, 54

Vogel, Vladimir, b. 1896, Russo-German composer, 184

Volbach, Fritz, 1861–1940, German composer, 184

Vuataz, Roger, b. 1898), composer, 184

Vuckovic, Vojislav, 1910–1942, Yugoslav composer, 184

W

Wachs, Paul, 19th century, Italian composer, 68

Wagenaar, Johan, 1862–1941, Dutch composer, 118

Wagner, Richard, 68 [unidentified arranger, march from *Tannhäuser*]; 199 [arranged for band by Stokowsky]; 205

Wagner, Eugéne, 19th century composer, 196

Wagner, J. F., 19th century composer, 200

Wagner, P. Basilius, d. 1813 at Melk [dedication], 59

Wagner, Siegfried Richard, 1869–1930, German composer, 118, 184

Wailly, Paul de, fl. 1882–1900, French composer, 192

Walter, Karl, 1862–1929, Austrian composer, 118

Weber, Bernhard Anselm, 1766–1821, German composer, 44

Weber, Carl Maria von, 1786–1826, German composer, 43, 54 [*Der Freischütz*, arranged by Flachs for Harmoniemusik], 205

Weber, Ludwig, 1891–1947, German composer, 119, 184

Wehrli, Werner, 1892–1944, Swiss composer, 119, 185

Weichowicz, Stanislaw, b. 1893, Polish composer, 119

Weigl, Josef, Austrian, 1766–1846, *Die Uniform*, arr. unidentified arranger for Harmoniemusik, 54

Weill, Kurt, 1900–1950, German composer, 119

Weinzweig, John, b. 1913, Canadian composer, 119, 185

Weis, Flemming, b. 1898, Danish composer, 185

Weismann, Julius, 1879–1950, German composer, 185

Weissensteiner, Raimund, b. 1905, Austrian composer, 185

Wellesz, Egon, b. 1885, Austrian composer, 186

Wendt, Giovanni, Austrian composer, 1745–1809, 34

Wenzel, Eberhard, b. 1896, German, 186

Whittaker, William Gillies, 1876–1944, English, 186

Whitwell, David, 20th century conductor, composer, 205

Widmer, Ernst, Brazilian 20th century composer, 205

Widor, 19th century French composer, 212

Wieprecht, Wilhelm, 1802–1872, German composer and conductor, 62, 68

Wieweg, 20th century publisher in Berlin, 123

Wildgans, Friedrich, 1913–1965, German composer, 120

Wilhelm I of Germany, 19th century, [dedication], 61

Wilhelm, 19th century Prince of Prussia, 68

Willi, 20th century publisher in Cham, 88

Winter, Paul, 1894–1971, German composer, 120

Winter, Peter von, Austrian composer, 1754–1825, 44, 53 [*Das unterbrochene*, arranged for Harmoniemusik by Stumpf]; 54 [*Vologesus* (ballet), unidentified arranger of Harmoniemusik]

Wirth, Helmut, b. 1912, German composer, 186

Wiss, H. B., 19th century French, composer, 69

Witmann, G., French, 19th century band conductor, 69

Wittelsbach, Rudolf, b. 1902, composer, 186

Wittmann, J. B., French, 19th century band conductor, 69

Woestijne, David van de, b. 1915, Belgian composer, 186

Wohlfahrt, Frank, b. 1894, German composer, 120, 187

Wood, Ralph, b. 1901, composer, 187

Wood, Ralph, b. 1901, English composer, 120

Wood, Thomas, 1892–1950, English composer, 120

Wöss, Josef Venantius von, 1863–1943, Austrian composer, 120

Woyrsch, Felix, 1860–1944, German composer, 187

Woytowicz, Boleslaw, b. 1899, Polish composer, 187

Wynne, David, b. 1900, Welsh composer, 187

Z

Zabala, Nicola, 19th century Italian composer, 69

Zbinden, Julien-François, b. 1917, Swiss composer, 120

Zender, Hans, b. 1936, German composer, 121, 187

Zenemükiadó Vállalat, 20th century publisher in Budapest, 159

Zerboni, S., 20th century publisher in Milan, 175

Zetter, 19th century publisher in Paris, 66

Ziegler, Benno, 1891–1965, German composer, 121

Zillig, Winfried, 1905–1963, German composer, 121, 187

Zöllner, Richard, b. 1896, German composer, 188

Zoras, Leonidas, b. 1905, Greek composer, 121

About the Author

DR. DAVID WHITWELL is a graduate ('with distinction') of the University of Michigan and the Catholic University of America, Washington DC (PhD, Musicology, Distinguished Alumni Award, 2000) and has studied conducting with Eugene Ormandy and at the Akademie für Musik, Vienna. Prior to coming to Northridge, Dr. Whitwell participated in concerts throughout the United States and Asia as Associate First Horn in the USAF Band and Orchestra in Washington DC, and in recitals throughout South America in cooperation with the United States State Department.

At the California State University, Northridge, which is in Los Angeles, Dr. Whitwell developed the CSUN Wind Ensemble into an ensemble of international reputation, with international tours to Europe in 1981 and 1989 and to Japan in 1984. The CSUN Wind Ensemble has made professional studio recordings for BBC (London), the Köln Westdeutscher Rundfunk (Germany), NOS National Radio (The Netherlands), Zürich Radio (Switzerland), the Television Broadcasting System (Japan) as well as for the United States State Department for broadcast on its 'Voice of America' program. The CSUN Wind Ensemble's recording with the Mirecourt Trio in 1982 was named the 'Record of the Year' by The Village Voice. Composers who have guest conducted Whitwell's ensembles include Aaron Copland, Ernest Krenek, Alan Hovhaness, Morton Gould, Karel Husa, Frank Erickson and Vaclav Nelhybel.

Dr. Whitwell has been a guest professor in 100 different universities and conservatories throughout the United States and in 23 foreign countries (most recently in China, in an elite school housed in the Forbidden City). Guest conducting experiences have included the Philadelphia Orchestra, Seattle Symphony Orchestra, the Czech Radio Orchestras of Brno and Bratislava, The National Youth Orchestra of Israel, as well as resident wind ensembles in Russia, Israel, Austria, Switzerland, Germany, England, Wales, The Netherlands, Portugal, Peru, Korea, Japan, Taiwan, Canada and the United States.

He is a past president of the College Band Directors National Association, a member of the Prasidium of the International Society for the Promotion of Band Music, and was a member of the founding board of directors of the World Association for Symphonic Bands and Ensembles (WASBE). In 1964 he was made an honorary life member of Kappa Kappa Psi, a national professional music fraternity. In September, 2001, he was a delegate to the UNESCO Conference on Global Music in Tokyo. He has been knighted by sovereign organizations in France, Portugal and Scotland and has been awarded the gold medal of Kerkrade, The Netherlands, and the silver medal of Wangen, Germany, the highest honor given wind conductors in the United States, the medal of the Academy of Wind and Percussion Arts (National Band Association) and the highest honor given wind conductors in Austria, the gold medal of the Austrian Band Association. He is a member of the Hall of Fame of the California Music Educators Association.

Dr. Whitwell's publications include more than 127 articles on wind literature including publications in Music and Letters (London), the London Musical Times, the Mozart-Jahrbuch (Salzburg), and 39 books, among which is his 13-volume *History and Literature of the Wind Band and Wind Ensemble* and an 8-volume series on *Aesthetics in Music*. In addition to numerous modern editions of early wind band music his original compositions include 5 symphonies.

David Whitwell was named as one of six men who have determined the course of American bands during the second half of the 20th century, in the definitive history, *The Twentieth Century American Wind Band* (Meredith Music).

A doctoral dissertation by German Gonzales (2007, Arizona State University) is dedicated to the life and conducting career of David Whitwell through the year 1977. David Whitwell is one of nine men described by Paula A. Crider in *The Conductor's Legacy* (Chicago: GIA, 2010) as 'the legendary conductors' of the 20th century.

'I can't imagine the 2nd half of the 20th century—without David Whitwell and what he has given to all of the rest of us.' Frederick Fennell (1993)

About the Editor

CRAIG DABELSTEIN began studying the piano at age seven and took up the saxophone at age twelve. Mr Dabelstein has Bachelor of Arts (Music) and Bachelor of Music degrees from the Queensland Conservatorium of Music, where he majored in the performance of classical saxophone repertoire. He also has a Graduate Diploma of Learning and Teaching and a Graduate Certificate in Editing and Publishing from the University of Southern Queensland.

He has held the principal alto and tenor saxophone chairs in the Australian Wind Orchestra and has been an augmenting member of the Queensland Philharmonic Orchestra, the Queensland Symphony Orchestra, and the Queensland Pops Orchestra. For many years he was also a member of the Queensland Saxophone Quartet.

He has been a casual conductor of the Young Conservatorium Symphonic Winds, and has previously been a saxophone teacher at the Queensland Conservatorium of Music. He is a regular conductor of the Queensland Wind Orchestra, having served as their artistic director and chief conductor from 2004 to 2009.

Craig Dabelstein is a research associate for the *Teaching Music Through Performance in Band* series of books, contributing analyses to volumes 7, 8, 1 (rev. edn), and the *Solos with Wind Band Accompaniment* volume. He served as the copyeditor and layout designer of the *Australian Clarinet and Saxophone Magazine* from 2007 to 2009 and he has written many CD and book reviews for *Music Forum* magazine. He is the editor of the second editions of the books by Dr. David Whitwell including *A Concise History of the Wind Band, Foundations of Music Education, Music Education of the Future, The Sousa Oral History Project, Wagner on Bands, Berlioz on Bands, The Art of Musical Conducting,* and the *Aesthetics of Music* series (8 volumes) and *The History and Literature of the Wind Band and Wind Ensemble* series (13 volumes). From 1994 to 2012 he was a staff member at Brisbane Girls Grammar School. He now teaches woodwinds and conducts bands at St. Joseph's College, Gregory Terrace, Brisbane.

www.ingramcontent.com/pod-product-compliance
Lightning Source LLC
Chambersburg PA
CBHW080417270326
41929CB00018B/3056